MW01098325

To the memory
of John Madson
1923-1995

Pheasant Tales

PHEASANT TALES

Original Stories About
America's Favorite Game Bird

John Barsness ■ Philip Bourjaily
Chris Dorsey ■ Jim Fergus ■ Steve Grooms
Gene Hill ■ Tom Huggler ■ Jay Johnson
Robert F. Jones ■ Randy Lawrence ■ John Madson
Michael McIntosh ■ Steve Stallard
Charles F. Waterman

Illustrations by Eldridge Hardie

Doug Truax and Art DeLaurier Jr., editors

Countrysport Press
New Albany, Ohio

This edition of *Pheasant Tales* was printed by Jostens Book Manufacturing, State College, Pennsylvania. The book was designed by Angela Saxon of Saxon Design, Traverse City, Michigan. The text is set in Berkeley Book.

© 1995 by Countrysport, Inc.
Illustrations © 1995 by Eldridge Hardie

First Edition
10 9 8 7 6 5 4 3 2 1

Published by Countrysport Press
15 South High Street, New Albany, Ohio 43054-0166

Printed in the United States of America

Library of Congress Cataloging-in-Publication Data
Pheasant tales : original stories about America's favorite game bird /
    John Barsness ... [et al.] ; illustrations by Eldridge Hardie ;
    introduction by Jay Johnson. — 1st ed.
        p.   cm.
    ISBN 0-924357-55-X
    1. Pheasant shooting—United States. 2. Ring-necked pheasant—
United States.   I. Barsness, John.
SK325.P5P48 1995
799.2'48617—dc20   95-20962
                                                              CIP

CONTENTS

INTRODUCTION
Art DeLaurier Jr. _____ vii

1 FREAK PHEASANTS
Charles F. Waterman _____ 3

2 ONE BIRD AT A TIME
Philip Bourjaily _____ 17

3 PHEASANTS WEST OF THE 100TH
John Barsness _____ 33

4 GLORIOUS CARNAGE
Robert F. Jones _____ 47

5 TEN-SECOND PHEASANTS
Gene Hill _____ 65

6 PHEASANT GUNS AND GUNNING
Michael McIntosh _____ 73

7 FORTY YEARS OF PHEASANT HUNTING
Tom Huggler _____ 89

8 FOOTPRINTS IN THE SNOW
Chris Dorsey _____ 107

9 FIELD TRIPS
Steve Grooms _____ 119

10 HOME TO ROOST
Randy Lawrence _____ 133

11 THE PHEASANT QUEST
Jim Fergus _____ 147

12 A TASTE OF WILDNESS
Steve Stallard _____ 159

13 PHEASANTS FOREVER
Jay Johnson _____ 173

14 PHEASANTS BEYOND AUTUMN
John Madson _____ 181

INTRODUCTION

by Art DeLaurier Jr.

In 1881, Judge Owen Denny shanghaied thirty Chinese ring-necked pheasants and shipped them to Oregon. Of those thirty, twenty-six survived to be released in the Willamette Valley, marking the first successful attempt at introducing the ringneck to North America. Others followed suit, and in just a few years, the pheasant gained a strong foothold in the New World, ranging from coast to coast throughout the northern United States.

A combination of suitable habitat (the right mix of native grasses and agriculture) and a little boost from state game departments (artificial breeding and stocking) contributed to the pheasant explosion that followed. In 1927, South Dakota alone reported a bag of approximately 2 million birds, a record that, like Ty Cobb's hit total, seemed at the time impossible to break. Of course, no one could forecast the coming pheasant-hunters' heaven—the Soil Bank days of the 1940s, '50s, and '60s—when millions of acres of crop-lands were retired and South Dakota broke its own record with 3.2 million birds taken in a single season.

The 1970s saw an end to the glut of the Soil Bank days. Secretary of Agriculture Earl Butz's fencerow-to-fencerow farm-ing policy led to the decimation of pheasant habitat, and bird numbers throughout the country plummeted, remaining low until the Conservation Reserve Program (CRP) passed with the 1985 Farm Bill and once again idled millions of acres of farmland.

Today, thanks to CRP and conservation groups like the seventy-thousand-member Pheasants Forever, the ring-necked pheasant is making a comeback in states like Minnesota and Michigan, where bird numbers had previously dwindled, and holding its own in states like Iowa and South Dakota, which boasts a current population of 5 million birds.

That's the short, plain history of pheasants in this coun-try. Graphed it might look like a steady climb to the first big hill on a roller coaster—the apex, the swift descent, the smaller hills. But it's really not all that exciting. You can read a more detailed account in any ornithological history of gallinaceous birds, but don't—unless you're looking for a quick cure for insomnia. The real history of the ring-necked pheasant is in the stories that follow. It's in the stories of the men who hunt them, the men who know them best.

Take, for instance, Tom Huggler's personal account of "Forty Years of Pheasant Hunting," in which he writes about his first hunt. In one poignant moment he is told by his father to dispatch a wounded bird with his Red Ryder BB gun. He does so and writes: "My father's rooster is now my rooster. It is a bird as beautiful in death as it was in life: the painted head with its blood-red cheek patches, sleek crown of emerald, white throat ring.

The black-tipped bronze breast feathers changing like an oil slick from purple to green to blue."

One bird, so many colors. That might as well be the theme of this book. It was the poet William Blake who wrote: "As a man is, so he sees; as the eye is formed, thus are its proportions." Though the writers in this book share the ringneck's general history, each has a unique and individual relationship with pheasants. Each has an eye of his own, and each has a voice that has caught and sang these birds in flight.

There's Charley Waterman, veteran of many ringneck sorties, recalling some of his stranger encounters: a hunt, as he says, "in which there were *too many* pheasants"; his famed Brittany Kelley's secret approach to hunting ringnecks; the burly Kaiser's own unconventional method of flushing roosters.

Gene Hill, with his usual conciseness, combines a lesson in shooting with the poetry of the western plains: covered wagons, wild buffalo, Sioux warriors, and arrowheads.

John Barsness, who writes plaintively about the vanishing West, the decline of "secret places" to hunt wild pheasants in Montana, and the voices that say "there's no place for grizzly bears." As he puts it, "when grizzlies go, wild pheasants won't be far behind."

Jim Fergus, whose quest for wild birds leads him around the world and back to the native species of his homeland. His, too, is a cry for wildness: "Wild birds, wild lands, forever!"

Phil Bourjaily, who traces the pheasant's rough-and-tumble history, recalls some of his own hunts, and tells how the ringneck has earned the right to be counted one bird at a time.

And there's Tom Huggler, who relates his own personal history of chasing longtails—in the heartland and in the heart.

Veteran wingshooter and gun expert Michael McIntosh tells you all you need to know about John Ringneck, and the guns, loads, and methods needed to bring him down.

Robert F. Jones, whose chapter "Glorious Carnage," which recounts a pheasant drive during the golden age of the Soil Bank era and a driven shoot in England, reads like a lesson out of Clausewitz's book of military strategy.

Chris Dorsey, who recalls how the slightest thing—new snow, a dog bell, a cold wind—takes him back to his first hunt.

Steve Grooms writes about a man who taught a hunter education class for troubled inner-city youths that everyone else had given up on; how a little faith turned into a fantastic pheasant season.

Randy Lawrence, whose story tells how the shame of his first hunt turns a young man away from pheasants—for a time. Find out how it's the small, good things that lead to redemption.

Executive Chef Steve Stallard, who gives recipes for aging, preparing, and cooking pheasants in a way that preserves and enhances their natural flavors.

Jay Johnson, Pheasants Forever's director of special projects, who profiles his organization's conservation efforts, examines the current state of ringneck affairs, and gives advice on how we can all work to preserve our pheasant hunting heritage.

And finally, the late John Madson, whose chapter, "Pheasants Beyond Autumn," explores how late-season pheasants offer the greatest challenges and the greatest rewards. We thought it timeless enough to include in this original anthology and are sure you will too.

Enjoy.

CHARLES F. WATERMAN

Charles F. Waterman says he quit honest work shortly after World War II and has been a freelance outdoor writer for nearly fifty years. Before that war he was a newspaper writer and photographer, and during it he skippered a Steichen combat photo team with the Navy in the Pacific. He was raised on a Kansas farm, wrote his first outdoor column in 1934, and has written seventeen hunting and fishing books, some of which, he says, disappeared without a ripple. He says that at one point when he and his wife Debie were faced with starvation he taught literature for a year at Stetson University. Their house is in Florida, but for more than thirty years they have spent summer and part of the fall in Montana.

one

FREAK PHEASANTS

by Charles F. Waterman

oth pheasants and pheasant hunters are a little hard to classify. I have seen pheasant hunters in ragged bib overalls and some with neckties, which, I understand, is routine in Europe. I have seen pheasants scooting between desert cactus plants, wading through swamps, jumping off mountains, and hiding in tool sheds.

My point is that if I should relate some rather unusual pheasant hunting situations, I hope they will be received as fact and may be accepted as educational material rather than as the bemused babblings of one who has been surprised by too many pheasants. For example, there are skeptical souls who might doubt that I have participated in a pheasant hunt in which there were *too many* pheasants, as was the case when the rancher grinned, looked at my expectant pointer, and told me to go ahead and hunt.

"That draw is full of them!" he said. "They're squawking all the time!"

In more recent years, most western agriculturists are less generous with the pheasant supply and have noted the fact that pheasants can be a pretty good cash crop.

But on the day I speak of, two of us with two bird dogs approached the ravine in question with considerable anticipation, made sure the safeties were where we had left them, and smiled happily as one Brittany and one pointer posed rigidly just outside a brushy jungle. A morning breeze brought us a strong scent familiar to anyone who had been reared on a farm with a large poultry population.

"Must be a million of them!" Frank said.

The dogs continued to point and we stumbled into the cover. The damp ground was a solid pattern of pheasant tracks and I heard the scuffle of pheasant feet ahead. The dogs changed position and pointed again.

Now those of us who have pursued certain quail species often speak importantly of "covey dogs" and "singles dogs," but our situation could not have been improved by any pointing specialty. Of course, what we needed was a really wild-eyed flush dog or two, but even that wouldn't really solve the problem, for that's what our classy young pointing geniuses became within a few minutes. It didn't do them any harm, I guess, for they were pointing fairly steadily again in only a couple of months.

I have no idea how many pheasants were in that draw but I am sure they could have won if they had rushed us. Since then I have thought of that place whenever I am very tired, the sun is almost down, I have no birds, I am not quite sure where the truck is, and my dog has pointed a skunk.

Although there are thousands of pheasant hunters who do it without dogs, most of my operations have involved dogs of various types and sizes, usually of the pointing breeds. Some of them have been pheasant specialists, and others have sought pheasants on demand although they preferred more conventional species. Some of the most interesting of these dogs have sought pheasants as a hobby although they made their living with things

like ruffed grouse or quail. Your true pheasant hobbyist invariably develops unique approaches, comes as near giggling as a canine can, and is delighted at finding a kindred soul among humans. My own Brittany, Kelly, was a hobbyist all the way from puppyhood to old age and worked out some special tactics for pheasants while retaining a more conventional approach for other game. He never learned to bay cornered pheasants but he developed a yipping program that worked very well on numerous occasions. The yipping approach was completely Kelly's own plan and he introduced me to it one day in a slough that divided an enormous field of wheat stubble and provided cover for an indeterminate number of pheasants.

Although pointing dogs are supposed to "slam into points," the pheasant genius is likely to gumshoe or sneak into points, as Kelly often did. These points likely occurred when a rooster was sliding along ahead through some heavy cover, and Kelly's yipping approach took me by surprise one day when he had been into the pheasant game only a couple of years. Apparently Kelly was following a rooster, and I was following Kelly, who was building tension with his usual unspoken over-the-shoulder pheasant commentary. He did that with rolling eyes, a conspiratorial grin, and an attitude that said plainly, "Man, he's here and you better be ready!"

Then Kelly stopped in his version of a staunch point and I swished up behind him through some grass and scattered briars. I assumed our quarry had stopped running but knew it might resume travel momentarily. I was alongside Kelly and we were stock-still for a second before he jumped straight up in the air and yipped, a procedure which was too much for a pheasant rooster, even one that may have intended to pause only briefly, and it flushed with the full, squawking, clattering treatment. I shot it.

Not everyone appreciates such subtle approaches. My friend was standing fifty yards to one side in the hope that something would come his way.

"What the hell was all that?" he asked.

It is difficult to classify pheasant dogs. At one time I tried to list them as either sneaky or violent, but that has not worked out as some of the more advanced operators change attitude with the individual situation. Let us state, however, that few flush dogs are sneaky, and veteran pheasant pointing dogs often change tactics with the situation.

German shorthaired pointers have long held a high position in pheasant ratings, a matter that should be soft-pedaled around owners of other breeds. In seeking a basis for this reputation, I studied a scientific treatise on dog intelligence and found the German shorthair listed as the brainiest of all pointers. This, of course, is based on a set of tests obviously spurious to owners of other breeds, but I believe shorthair acumen is keyed toward pheasants, as in the case of Kaiser, a dog who worked with a friend of mine. Personally, I was not particularly fond of Kaiser as I felt he thought he was better than I was, but I was impressed by his pheasant approach.

"We have a whole lot of ditches around here," Kaiser's associate confided. "Kaiser specializes in those where there are old weeds that lie flat. He points straight down after he walks around and finds the roosters are running around under him."

Kaiser did not walk very fast but he kept his ears pricked as if listening for pheasant footsteps beneath him, and if the weeds were heavy enough and flat enough he would, indeed, point straight down. A pheasant coming out from under seventy pounds of dog and a layer of flattened weeds was immediately noticeable.

Although Kaiser's method was hardly classic, it was dainty compared to that of Bones, a burly ranch dog with no known breed affiliation.

"Where he comes from I think it is sort of a survival of the fittest," Jack said. "When we got him he was just passing through but he sure moves the pheasants!"

No, Jack said, he did not know what Bones weighed because no one had volunteered to put him on the scales.

"But he's pretty big," Jack said. "None of the neighbors' dogs come around anymore."

Jack and I took Bones to what Jack said was a fine "pheasant patch." It was a slough with ice, snow, cattails, and some thorny bushes.

"Actually," Jack said, "Bones does not really *hunt* pheasants. He inaugurates pheasant migrations."

We stumbled along the edge of the heavy cover while Bones smashed through it, woofing threateningly from time to time, and driving out various rabbits, one skunk, a white-tailed deer, and both sexes of pheasants. When we shot one pheasant, Jack said Bones might bring it to us but not to discuss it with him.

"If you call his attention to a dead bird," Jack said, "he might take offense, thinking you are interfering with his business, and he might carry it off into the really thick stuff."

When the hunt was finished, Jack said pheasants might be back in the slough again in a couple of weeks.

Lest you get the impression I am dealing mainly with the less refined types of pheasant-seeking canines, I should report that I am known to write about the training aspects of all sorts of bird dogs, some of them true specialists. Of late, there are more and more pheasant shooters who follow dogs on preserves, and they may do so with limited time and a businesslike approach.

I had an inquiry from a man who said he needed to adjust the range of his pointer, which he used solely on pheasants. Reducing the range of hard-charging bird dogs is a common problem and I needed details. Just how far did he want his dog to range?

"Range? What do you mean, range?" he snapped. "I plant these birds myself and I know exactly where each one is, and when I go to one, I want my dog to point it and I don't want him fooling around twenty-five or thirty feet away."

I suggested that he try a short lead and he has not called back.

Although they seldom mention it, true pheasant hunters generally know that the ringneck was not here when Europeans first arrived, but then the first Europeans didn't have Churchill shotguns either. We know now that in addition to pheasants that have truly gone wild, there are a great many added to sweeten the pot, so to speak. Different strains perform in different ways but some of them, when dumped from a crate, are wild before they hit the ground. A few sit down and wait for feeding time.

Although I have taken some interest in the migrations of the Arctic tern and various ducks and geese, it is the travels of the freshly planted ringneck that really intrigue me. Jack, who established a precarious working relationship with the aforementioned Bones, lived on a ranch with plenty of pheasant cover, and he had pretty good shooting nearly every year but figured there was no such thing as an oversupply of birds. One year he told me he had swung a deal with some professional pheasant planters who were employed annually by a large sportsman's club and would release a thousand birds or so just before the season opened each year. After a clandestine meeting and some financial arrangements with the pheasant impresarios, Jack confided to me that a large share of the released roosters would be placed upon his land to supplement what he considered a minimal supply of birds.

On opening day, with all those waiting ringnecks, we didn't start especially early. It was not a day for Bones, the brush buster, as we were prepared with a pair of cultured and pheasant-wise pointing dogs. We began back of the corrals where Chinese roosters had been yelling at each other all year, but for some reason they were not present and a skift of snow showed they had really moved. It was late in the day with no pheasants sighted at all when Jack summarized the situation.

"It's those blamed hatchery pheasants!" Jack said. "Not only did they leave as soon as they decided they didn't like the place, but they took all of my birds with them."

It was not one of Jack's better pheasant seasons. He scoured the countryside for miles around, day after day, but found only an occasional bird that had apparently taken no part in the migration.

There are a variety of methods for shooting pheasants, driven birds being most socially acceptable and generally most expensive. Cultured gunners who have shot driven pheasants much of their lives sometimes imply that kicking a pheasant out of the mud and weeds and shooting at him from the rear is too easy and therefore unsportsmanlike. I have always felt this is a matter of the physical condition of the gunner. If he has been stumbling through freezing mud and snow for several hours and has had no shots at all, I feel that the going-away shot is sporty enough. And I consider shooting pheasants from duck blinds just as uplifting as waiting for them to cross a hedgerow with beaters in pursuit.

The duck blind business is not widely practiced but I had a sporting introduction to it when two of us built a shabby hideout along a creek that bordered a lot of pheasant cover. The mallard shooting was never very good there but it developed that when pheasant hunters were active upstream the escaping birds would fly right down the creek regularly.

We did not look good on the first few chances, not having planned such an operation. On the first occasion, Dave had just finished a one-sided conversation with some high-circling mallards and had settled back against the stump he used for a backrest when there was a hissing sound. There was an unidentified shadow that flicked across the blind interior, and after doing the manual of arms and finding no target, we spent a few minutes figuring what sort of duck had buzzed us and gone off laughing.

On the second chance a few days later, the pheasant gave us a close-up look, and as soon as I realized it was not a long-necked duck flying backward I made an artistic swing, taking out part of the crude blind and failing to decapitate the game, which squawked as it left.

"That," I said, "was a pheasant."

"It was a pheasant all right," Dave said, reloading his three-inch magnum.

I happened to be alone in the blind a few days later, and when I heard a distant cackle I began thinking pheasants. I sighted the bird more than a hundred yards upstream, obviously hugging the shoreline. I even had time for a practice point before the moment of truth and I killed a cock pheasant just across the creek, where it plopped on a patch of grass. After that, we accepted an occasional rooster as a logical part of a mallard and gadwall bag.

In keeping with my purpose in writing this treatise you will note that I do not cover the *traditional* aspects of pheasant hunting. Like others, I have walked up behind a pointing dog and had a pheasant climb out of the weeds with a lot of insulting noises and have, on occasion, been able to hit him. I have also participated in a similar program with a flushing dog. I have even stood at one end of a cornfield with a good supply of high-brass 6s and had friendly souls drive pheasants toward me and other would-be assassins. But I am trying to give you a view of the unusual angles of pheasant hunting.

Some believe the Chinese rooster's plumage is designed as an equalizing factor, the premise being that the bird is superior in intelligence and could not be kept under control if it were camouflaged like, say, a Wilson's snipe or a Mearns quail.

On a few occasions I have known the rooster's gaudy costume to cause him inconvenience or worse, as in the case of the one we sighted between the creek bottom and the stubble field. That creek bottom was a real bramble patch, perfect for pheasant roosting, and the grain field was easy pickings when a pheasant got hungry. Between the grain and the creek was a patch of overgrazed pasture that appeared sparse enough to challenge a starving goat. Pheasants could fly from the creek to the grain but occasionally they walked across the intervening wasteland. Maybe they found grasshoppers.

Even a sneaky old ringneck can make an error in judgment. There came a day when two of us took two shotguns and one pointer toward the brushy creek bottom, already complaining about thorns, marshy sinkholes, and cowardly roosters, and as we crossed the short-grass wasteland between the creek and the grain we saw a dark, moving spot far ahead. Could it be a pheasant was thus challenging fate?

Evidently a single rooster was out for a stroll between the grain and the brush, and we assumed he would simply voice oriental curses and fly back into the creek bottom, but he evidently felt lucky. There was a bucket-sized patch of prickly pear out there in the wide open, along with a little bouquet of scraggly grass, and he chose to hide in it. His tail stuck out a couple of feet.

As we gunners drew near, the pointer slowed down, probably blinked, and looked inquiringly at us. Then he pointed and looked at us again. He was in unfamiliar territory.

I would never bait pheasants with poison corn and, so far, have never blasted them on the ground, so I hope to have fulfilled my obligation to upland sportsmanship in most cases. Now, here was a dog pointing an overweight pheasant rooster in a two-foot patch of cover, and it was a matter of whether to take advantage of the situation or not. I stamped my foot, said "Boo!" and used high-brass No. 5s in an over-under 12-gauge shotgun.

Since pheasants have come from very distant parts of the world, it is obvious they can adapt to a wide variety of living conditions, even though there are certain parts of the country they refuse to accept. In discussing pheasant populations with biologists, I have found this is a delicate subject. In parts of the South the absence of pheasants has been a subject of honor, and when biologists sought to locate a kind of pheasant that would thrive where the conventional ringneck wouldn't, they came up with some pretty flamboyant types with brilliant hues and strange feather patterns. Before those colorful introductions disappeared entirely, it was not unusual for a palmetto-scarred pointer to find a gaudy feather duster instead of a bobwhite quail, resulting in a rumored increase in alcoholism among Florida gunners.

I am not surprised by pheasants as much as I used to be, having found my share of them in sagebrush where I expected sage grouse, and on mountains where I expected chukars. There was the time when three of us with a slavering Brittany approached a western creek where we'd found pheasants before.

This was no small-time operation. We intended to go up the creek, one of us on each side and one in the muddy middle, with the dog covering all of the good edges. He'd pointed a lot of pheasants and was willing to stalk a little if one wouldn't hold. He had pride but figured some classic form could be suspended in an emergency.

We began with me and the dog in the creek bottom, both of us receiving constant instructions from our associates on the high banks of the pastureland, both of them with dry boots and enthusiasm. We were working upstream. A pheasant hen clattered past me and went on downstream and the dog pointed and held another hen over against one of the high banks. Several more hens scuttled up the banks or flew off the way we had come.

"Nothing but hens left," Hugh said with the air of a man who is standing on high, dry ground and has a clear view of the situation. "This crick has been shot out. Probably crowded the first day of the season. Where else should we go?"

The walking got a little better, the creek was moving and looked clear, but we seemed to be out of the hens. I relaxed and thought how nice it would be to head downstream on dry ground. That is when I missed the rooster. He yelled a lot of pheasant things, flailed through the willows ahead of me, and went almost straight up. I shot over him just as he stopped going up and leveled off and Red whacked him.

The terrain had changed a little and our draw was turning into a canyon. Far ahead I caught a sight familiar to mountain pheasant chasers. It was a rooster charging up out of the creek bottom, sprinting between a couple of boulders and evidently headed for rimrock. There were no hens at all but roosters were running, squawking, flying, and climbing the canyon walls. We kept going until we had limits with a lot of canyon ahead of us. We ended our hunt and started back toward a toy ranch house far below.

"I'll show you plenty of pheasants," the man said, and he drove his truck into a broad western draw with all kinds of brush and a streak of willows in the bottom where there was a barely moving trickle of a creek.

He stopped the truck and the pheasants began to fly, just a few of them at first, hens and cocks, and then a curtain of pheasants, all headed up the draw on short flights. I finally found the door handle, stumbled out, and fumbled for my gun and shells. There was plenty of time, the man said.

"They're not going anywhere!" he explained, putting three pointing dogs on the ground. "We'll catch up with all of them we need."

The dogs began to work the pheasants—if dogs can be said to "work" herds of birds. Everything moved uphill, a re-newing flight seeming to roll ahead of us. But then, maybe there weren't as many as I thought. After the total reaches fifty or sixty I'm not too meticulous about pheasant counting.

As the draw began to narrow I began to see birds run-ning up out of the heavy brush and into little erosions on the shoulders of our bottom. Each one had a little patch of weeds and brush near the top—and farther on were stubble fields. We followed the dogs and the dogs followed the birds and pointed in the little patches of brush and weeds.

"How many are we going to shoot?" the man asked after spilling two cocks from the first patch. We quit early.

Back in Kansas where they tried to raise me on a farm, we didn't have pheasants and I got my first pheasant stories from people who went to places like Nebraska and South Dakota. Kansas pheasants were to come later. In the thirties I had a couple of friends who went to South Dakota in a roomy Stinson mono-plane with dogs and everything. And later, I got acquainted with Orville, who shot trap, skeet, quail, and waterfowl with slick-as-grease pumpguns. He was a gunsmith and said pheasants weren't very tough.

"I got twenty-two with twenty-three shells this year," he said. "I had to shoot one of them twice."

And when I got around to pheasants I found they were large, pretty slow, and very noisy. I found to my surprise that some of them escaped. I tried to keep that quiet among quail shooters and the like, for bobwhite quail can teeter off into the brush while I am picking which one to shoot at.

Unfortunately, I have by chance become associated with several notorious shotgunners, a couple of whom have been national champions. One of them shoots a full-choke gun for bobwhite quail, explaining that he uses the outer edge of the pattern for the first bird and gradually moves over into the middle as the covey recedes into the distance and he is on his third bird or so.

The fact is, I have missed quite a few pheasants—and not tower pheasants or over-the-hedgerow pheasants, but brush patch, jump-in-your-face pheasants. My feelings of inferiority increased when I became associated with a fellow who knocks off bobwhite quail in the casual way I'd dry-fire at a doorknob. Of course he can't tell you how he does it and I confided in him that I not only allowed an occasional quail to escape but I frequently missed pheasants.

"Oh, *pheasants!*" Bill said. "I can't hit pheasants! They blot out the skyline and yell like demons! A pheasant is kind of a flying freak!"

PHILIP BOURJAILY

Philip Bourjaily was born in Iowa City and has lived in the area all his life, with time out for high school in Barcelona, Spain, and college in Charlottesville, Virginia. After vigorously resisting his father's early attempts to turn him into a hunter, he took up the sport on his own after college and began writing about it shortly thereafter.

His work has appeared in Field and Stream, Sports Afield, The American Hunter, *and other national and regional publications. He is also co-author (with Vance Bourjaily) of the book* Fishing by Mail.

He lives in Iowa City with his wife, Pamela, sons Charles and John, and his German shorthaired pointer (ret.), Sam.

two

ONE BIRD AT A TIME

by Philip Bourjaily

ou could call it ersatz prairie or monoprairie, this 240-acre farm enrolled in the Conservation Reserve Program and planted to brome. Not exactly the sea of grass the first settlers encountered, but a good-sized man-made lake of it, anyway, and certainly as close to the real thing as I was going to get in Iowa in the mid-1990s. From my vantage point at the top of the wide, shallow draw I could see only waving stems to the east and a lone bur oak, survivor of prairie fires and miraculously spared by bulldozers. With my back to the cornfields of the next farm, and red-tailed hawks wheeling in the sky high above my head, I could imagine this land as it was before John Deere's moldboard plow ripped the native grasses up by their deep, strong roots. Maybe Sam will point me a prairie chicken, I thought fancifully.

Sam has a pretty sharp nose, but it's not good enough to pick up a trail one hundred years old. He tore through the grass, cataloged and dismissed its contents with one peremptory sniff, then veered behind me and disappeared. Shortly thereafter, his bell fell silent near the edge of the cornfield. I could follow my imagination, but Sam follows pheasants, and pheasants always lead us back to corn.

So yes, it was a ring-necked pheasant and not a prairie chicken that flushed when I kicked at the grass, and it was a 209 primer, not a percussion cap, that flashed when I pulled the trigger. There was no cloud of white smoke, either, to obscure my view of the rooster falling, just a hull flung sideways out of the action as the dog ran out to fetch him. Sam brought me the bird, and as I took it I could feel the flat-sided kernels of corn in its crop through the black-edged, iridescent neck feathers. What is improbable about the sight of a rooster pheasant in such a place is not the foreignness of the bird but instead how absolutely at home he seems—how perfectly his bright coloration blends with the grasses, how well he adapts to a diet of grain. When a glistening, long-tailed rooster flushes against the backdrop of a vast blue prairie sky, stubby wings beating hard to carry him cackling over the dried tan cornstalks, anyone can see then that corn and pheasants must have been made for one another; even though one came from Mexico, the other from Asia, both thrive in the midnight-black soil of the vanished prairies.

No one knows exactly what Judge Owen Denny had in mind when he introduced pheasants to Oregon in 1881. Whatever his vision of pheasants in America, it could not have included the sight of a lone hunter and his dog two thousand miles and 115 years away, standing knee-deep in grass the government had paid a farmer to grow instead of grain. Legend has it the ambassador developed a taste for pheasant while posted to Shanghai and wanted to enjoy the newfound delicacy upon his return to the states. Perhaps he thought of nothing more than keeping a few pheasants in the back yard to scratch at birdseed and grow plump until dragged to the cookhouse. Quite possibly, though, Judge Denny pictured himself and his friends dressed in aristocratic heather-mix tweeds, waiting in the butts with a loader and a pair of best guns as white-coated locals drove the birds to them. There might even have been lunch under canvas awnings afterwards—cider and cucumber sandwiches with the crusts trimmed off.

Denny was not the first American to bring pheasants to the New World. George Washington, among others, tried and

failed to stock birds (at Mt. Vernon) one hundred years before. Denny's was, nevertheless, the first successful attempt. The pheasants he planted in Oregon thrived and spread immediately, having ideas other than sticking around to play the captive fall guys in a New World version of the grand battue. Upon immigrating to America they found a land of opportunity, an erstwhile prairie conveniently planted to pheasant food. As the previous tenants, the prairie chickens, received their eviction notice via the plow, pheasants moved in and made themselves at home. Aided by game departments across the country, ringnecks soon flourished from Oregon to New York. In Iowa, the story goes, a storm in the winter of 1901 blew down fences at a game farm near Cedar Falls; two thousand birds took one look at the beckoning marshes, prairie grasses, and cornfields—ringneck paradise—and made a break for freedom, predating the first state pheasant stocking in Iowa by nine years.

By their peak in the 1940s, '50s, and '60s, just decades after their arrival, pheasants were as widespread and popular a game bird as we've ever had in this country. In 1944, Iowa held an emergency spring pheasant season to defend the vital wartime corn crop from ravenous pheasants and South Dakota's population was estimated at sixteen million birds. The formula for millions of pheasants is simple: grass and grain. Corn is a high energy birdseed that provides enough warmth to see pheasants through the coldest winter. Tall grasses, like the bluestem and switchgrass found in the prairies, shelter them from winter winds. Shorter grass—knee-high to us—provides nesting cover. From a pheasant's standpoint, trees represent only danger, providing convenient perches for hawks and owls.

It's tempting to think of pheasants solely as the classic American immigrant success story: opportunistic, possessed of a fierce will to survive, making a home thousands of miles from their native land through sheer grit and determination. In fact, pheasants today are wards of the agricultural state. The fencerow-to-fencerow farming policies of the 1970s changed the landscape from the right mix of corn and fallow ground to a sterile monoculture of cash crops. It may be difficult to imagine pheasants without corn, but it's depressingly easy to visualize corn without pheasants. You have only to visit parts of the Midwest flat enough to permit the most intensive kind of farming to see an endless expanse of black earth, a barren monotony unrelieved by fencelines, marshes, or grass. Or pheasants. They will never starve to death in corn country; even when the crops are plowed under there's plenty of waste grain to glean. But with no shelter in the winter and no safe place to nest, you have no birds.

The Conservation Reserve Program on the other hand, besides its many other benefits, has amounted to a virtual welfare program for pheasants. You'll hear no talk of taxpayer revolt from this bird hunter so long as my dollars are paying for pheasant cover. The ground idled under CRP protects pheasants from their deadliest summertime enemy, the mowing machine, which crushes nests and purees hens reluctant to leave their eggs during June hay cuttings. Wetlands and warm-season prairie grasses restored by the program provide ideal winter cover. Whether pheasants thrive or disappear from the United States in the twenty-first century depends less on their own up-by-the-spurstraps attitude and more on whatever farm policy becomes law in Washington, D.C.

While CRP has given birds a respite from the advance of modern agriculture, suburban growth has levied a harsh toll on ringneck populations in the East. A friend in Maryland recently hunted the entire season without seeing a single bird. Yet in great chunks of the Midwest pheasants remain ubiquitous. They perch on fenceposts, peck gravel on country roads, feed in farmer's windbreaks. In the spring, I've had cock birds fighting ten steps from my door. I once even watched a gallinaceous version of Pyramus and Thisbe as a rooster and hen courted in ardent frustration like the classical lovers separated from one another by a wall—in this case, the hog-tight fence in my back yard.

The wealth of birds in some places guarantees pheasant hunting remains accessible and affordable, a sport for the common man. One of the most dedicated pheasant hunters I know lives in a trailer, shoots a Remington 1100, carries a photo of his shorthair in his wallet, and repairs tires for a living. As long as he keeps every farmer's pickup in Iowa County aligned, balanced, and on the road, he'll never lack for places to hunt. Unable to tell a lug nut from a lamprey myself, I have even less to exchange for hunting rights: a handshake, common courtesy, and some venison salami or Christmas cookies at season's end. Almost always, around here, that's still the right price and I count myself very fortunate to live where I do. Already, though, the signs—as in "Hunting Rights Leased"— are growing ominous. Each year hunters who can pay a few thousand dollars for a season of hunting lock up more land. They and their apologists advance convincing arguments that their system benefits wildlife by giving farmers an economic incentive to manage land for game. Maybe so, but once the majority of hunters are priced out of the field, don't expect us to stand up for the hunting rights of the very few.

It's more difficult, nowadays, just finding landowners to ask permission from. The old generation of farmers—overalled men with two-toned, sun-weathered faces and hands knobby from half a century or more of close encounters with tractor hitches—worked full-time on the farm; you could always find them at home, wading around the hog lot or tinkering in the shed. Rural America is emptying out; now the farm often belongs to someone who lives in a town far away, and the farmhouse is rented, decaying, or torn down. The new generation of farmers till more ground with bigger equipment, renting three or four places, running from one to the next, and farming with a thoroughness that lays waste to bird cover. Those farmers who still work the home place take jobs in town as well, farming on evenings and weekends. Though no less generous than their parents, this new generation is a whole lot harder to track down when you want to ask permission. Loading up the car and driving into the country to knock on doors, as people used to do, proves only that farmers are a lot harder to find than pheasants.

For now, thankfully, pheasant hunting where I live remains very much the sport of the masses. Since our social system precludes the rounding up of villagers to serve as beaters, we of the Great Unwashed have had to invent other ways to flush Everyman's bird into gun range. Actually, not long ago a democratic version of the driven shoot dominated pheasant tactics. Overalls and 870s replaced tweeds and doubles and everyone carried a gun. One half of the group posted at the end of a field, the other marched toward them in a long line, sagging in the middle like a seine to keep birds from running around the ends. When the lines met, feathered sparks flew, magazines emptied in seconds, birds thumped to the ground—their long tails streaming behind—and shot pattered down among the cornstalks.

The mass drive and block has faded in popularity with pheasant hunters in recent years, although you'll still see it conducted on a smaller scale. Perhaps deer hunting, very much a gang affair in the Midwest, better suits those who have a taste for numbers and paramilitary organization in the field. Maybe the low bird populations of the early 1980s didn't provide the return on the manpower invested in a gang hunt. My cousin summed up those post–Earl Butz, pre-CRP days one afternoon as we bounced deer after deer out of the creek bottom where we searched vainly for pheasants: "The limit ought to be three deer a day and one pheasant a year, not the other way around."

Then, too, the cover has changed, from small, weedy cornfields to big, bare ones alongside equally large fields of set-aside grasses. There isn't a gang numerous enough to conduct a dragnet in a 120-acre field of grass. If there is, I want to be at least a county away when they start shooting. Whatever the reason, we hunt our birds now one at a time, rather than surrounding them by the dozen.

Take a drive through pheasant country today on a Saturday afternoon and you're much more likely to see three or four hunters walking abreast, with a busy, close-working dog quartering through the grass ahead of them. While they may or may not post a blocker, they'll nonetheless shoot most of their birds along the edge of the field, or in the corners, as birds pushed to the end of the cover must make a decision to hide or fly.

One solo, dogless hunter I know gangs up on birds all by himself, taking on the roles of driver and blocker more or less simultaneously. First, he posts noisily at one end of the cover, stamping his feet in place and talking loudly. Then he sneaks away from his stand, circles around to the other side of the field, and works back toward where he was—and where the birds believe he still is. Pheasants, he's convinced, won't run ahead and flush out of range if they think they're caught between two people.

If you hunt without a dog, such tactics, vigorously applied, will pay off just frequently enough to stave off complete discouragement. Having done a good deal of it myself in my earlier years, I'd rate hunting without canine assistance as only slightly more effective than chasing down pheasants and strangling them barehanded. One of the largest of the many frustrations of dogless hunting is having birds continually catch you off guard. When I walked up my own pheasants, I tiptoed nervously through the cover, anticipating the startling explosion of a rooster at my feet at any moment yet never fully ready for it. A white-knuckle grip on a gunstock, let me tell you, rarely promotes good shooting.

A pheasant on the ground can blend so well into his adopted habitat of grass and grain fields that you'll almost never even catch a glimpse of him as he runs through grass without a whisper, often not even disturbing the stems. When I do see a cock pheasant on the ground, head down, back hunched, tail held low, skulking through the grass, he looks to me exactly like a black cat, and he travels every bit as quietly. Even as modern farming irons out more and more of the wrinkles and folds in the landscape of their adopted home, pheasants slink with remarkable stealth through those fringes that remain, hiding themselves artfully in road ditches, clipped fields, and creek bottoms plowed to within an inch of the bank.

Without a dog to root these birds out, you'll walk past them. Where the gangs of yesterday hunted largely without dogs, today you might get the impression that the state issues German shorthairs along with small-game licenses if you take a survey of the dogs in the field on opening day. While I hunt over shorthairs myself, I'd never presume to criticize any breed, except perhaps to wish that Brittanies had tails. Pointers, flushers, close workers, or big runners, all can make fine pheasant dogs, given enough experience on wild birds. Any dog can find pheasants much, much better than I can.

Once, having asked permission to hunt a new farm sight-unseen, I arrived to find it planted entirely to brome grass and mowed down to around ankle height. The cover was too short, obviously, to hold birds, but off we went anyway. Now that Sam has retired, I've exchanged my own bony, humorless, high-strung, wide-ranging shorthair for a loaner model in the field: another shorthair, Alex, the Dog with Two Brains. Al, like a stegosaurus, has a tiny walnut-sized brain in his skull, plus an enlarged nerve bundle somewhere in his hips to keep his tail wagging constantly. Round and happy, no genius even by dog standards, Alex is going strong at ten years old and has learned a beautiful light touch with running birds that belies his draft horse gait and clownish nature.

As we made our way across the field Al kept looking back at me quizzically, wondering if he was supposed to run or hunt in this cover that even he could see would never hold a bird. I trailed uncertainly behind him, thinking perhaps I should have left the gun in the car and brought binoculars or a camera instead.

Alex suddenly jerked to a halt, undoubtedly pointing a mouse out of boredom. I leaned over to look in front of his nose, and the unseen rooster popped out of the short grass as if from a hole in the ground, all three feet of him suddenly materializing a foot or so from my face. Startled, I jumped back and missed twice. Never one to turn and glower with a reproachful look as some dogs will, Alex just loped fifteen yards and promptly stuck another bird. This one I hit, and he had the long spurs of a rooster who'd grown old by hiding in places most hunters never looked.

For all their wiles on the ground, pheasants in the air know nothing of stealth or evasive maneuvers; they set a straight course and hammer away furiously, cackling as often as not, just in case you hadn't already noticed them. A friend of my father's—a fine wingshot and diehard waterfowler—invariably refused to accompany Dad on pheasant hunts. "You like shooting kites?" he'd scoff. Perhaps hitting a rooster over a dog is easy, but don't dismiss pheasants as easy to kill on the wing. A cock flying across an open field has only the armor of his coppery feathers and pure spite to protect him, yet often that's enough. Like Cape Buffalo, pheasants at times turn inexplicably bulletproof. Fortunately, the similarity ends there, pheasants having neither horns nor a tendency to charge. If they did, I'd have long since been trampled into the stubble.

The same gun, choke, and load combination that folds one rooster may cause the next to barely miss a wingbeat. One day last season I centered a straightaway rooster with a charge of high-velocity 4s at thirty yards. Upon absorbing roughly fifteen times his body weight in pellet energy he staggered in the air, gathered himself up, and flew on with hardly a feather out of place. He'd still be going, too, if he hadn't flown into a fence and broken his neck on the top strand of barbed wire.

The pheasant's toughness makes a strong case for the 12-gauge as the mandatory ringneck gun. While a driven-game shooter would envision a 12 as a lightweight, open-bored double with a pair of light loads in its short chambers, a heavier, mass-produced repeater firing high-velocity fare is de rigueur in much of pheasant country. I shoot a gun of each type myself: one a trim over-under of moderately high grade, with improved-cylinder and modified chokes, and a repaired stock that rules out the use of heavy loads; the other, a modern, Japanese-made pump outweighing the double by a good pound, and roll-engraved with two pheasants flying over what I can only assume to be Mt. Fuji on the receiver.

The over-under is my father's old pheasant gun and one of those racy straight-hand doubles that cries out to be pointed and swung the moment you touch its richly figured stock. I hunt with it more often than not, since it adds a touch of distinction to my ordinary field outfit: plenty of blaze orange (so no one will shoot me) over Carhartts (social camouflage, to fool people into thinking I actually work for a living). Besides, the Beretta carries easily, reminds me of my father, and is pretty to look at when the birds aren't cooperating. All that aside, if I actually had to live on the pheasants I shot, I'd take the pump every time, with a modified tube in the barrel and $3\frac{3}{4}$-dram, $1\frac{1}{4}$-ounce loads of hard 5s in the chamber and two more up the magazine tube. Better yet, if feeding my family was my sole reason for hunting, I'd trade the pump in on a soft-kicking gas autoloader and shoot short magnums.

An English-style pheasant shooter might sneer at our repeaters as being unsporting, then in the same breath claim that no magazine gun can fire as quickly as a man with a loader and two London best doubles. So is the autoloader too fast or too slow? Secretly, I believe if the British had invented the 1100 themselves, they wouldn't shoot anything else. However, pull the forearm off that most American of shotguns, the 11-87, and you'll see a design that could have sprung only from the mind of a Yankee tinkerer —valves, cylinders, rings, and pistons, a miniature internal combustion engine arrayed along the magazine tube. Having watched a college roommate smitten by the sleek beauty and deft handling of a British sports car go broke and slowly insane trying to keep it running, I can only imagine the expensive nightmare of owning, say, a London best autoloader, if such an unlikely gun were ever to exist.

The debate about which shoots faster, one auto or two doubles, is really moot since very few hunters can afford to buy bespoke doubles, much less pay to feed a loader. Besides, in our "rough shooting" style of hunting, we rarely flush pheasants in numbers that would require someone standing close by with a pair of guns. Doubles do happen, and triples are not unheard of—but neither is being struck by lightning. Mostly, we shoot our birds with intervals of hours, even days, between shots. I've only once seen pheasants flush in waves and fly exactly as they should on a properly conducted English driven shoot. Appropriately enough, I saw it from the beater's viewpoint, since most of us, when we fantasize about living in other times, conveniently ignore the odds when we arrange to have ourselves born into the shooting, not the beating, classes.

On that day, late last season, my cousin and I pulled into a snowy cornfield where three terraces of heavy grass on a south-facing hill promised to hold birds on a bitter December afternoon. The sight of half a dozen pheasants eating corn by the gate didn't hurt our chances, either. As the six birds flushed and flew into the terraces, we briefly debated the merits of splitting up so that one of us could block the far end, at the top of the hill. Too casual a team to waste time planning, we decided to turn all three dogs loose and see what happened.

A single blocker would have been hopelessly outnumbered, perhaps even overrun. At the very least, he'd have blistered his fingers on his gun barrels. If ever there were an occasion to have twelve titled shooters waiting in waxed cotton with pairs of Holland and Holland shotguns, this was it. As the dogs charged across the hillside, intoxicated by the scent of massed game birds, pheasants flushed from the terraces in wave after wave of a dozen or more birds, as driven pheasants are supposed to do. They climbed high to rise over a small woodlot, gliding and sideslipping over the treetops. The gamekeeper would have posted the guns on the far side of the woods and been tipped handsomely for his skill at presenting high, challenging targets.

No matter how tricky the shooting, the sports waiting in the butts would have missed the real fun. Chasing the dogs across the terraces, we tried to home in on their three bells, each one leading in a different direction. Guided by the tinkling, we'd hear the dogs tracking, then pointing in the tall grass, then breaking as another flock of birds streamed up into the sky, these late-season birds being far too spooky to sit still for long. Shaun and I dashed from flush to flush, trying futilely to catch up to a straggler.

Pausing to mop my brow, I looked down and saw Sam's tracks in the snow, identifiable as always by the faint drops of blood from his thin foot pads. I began to follow, and saw the paw-prints single out a particular set of pheasant tracks. The trail showed plainly where the pheasant had tried to double back, where it sat tight for a second, then sprinted full-out, the relentless dog always trailing just far enough behind so as not to bump the pheasant into flight. I found the two locked together at the end of the terrace. Sam had swung around to cut the bird off and stood immobile at the edge of the grass, barring escape in the direction the other pheasants had gone. With several acres of chest-high switchgrass to his back, however, this rooster was far from trapped. The dog's tail began to flag, and I saw a flicker of movement against the snow as the bird skulked away. I took two quick steps in the pheasant's direction and he flushed, straight up, inches from my face, then curled back over my head. Not one to ooze sangfroid when pheasants are on the wing, I turned and waited with surprising calm for the rooster to widen the gap between us, and dropped the only bird of the day hard into the snow.

That pheasant made dinner for two, with lunch left over and bones for stock—more than reward enough for a day's hunt. Besides, each of the fifty or so roosters that escaped over the trees might lead us on another breathless chase before the season ended. My entire year's bag doesn't equal one gun's pickup after a good drive in England, Hungary, or Czechoslovakia, but I prize each bird that much more for its scarcity and individuality. If I concentrate, I can remember every single pheasant I've ever killed. That much seems the very least I owe these imports who fill my autumn days in a land where prairie chickens and ruffed grouse are ghosts, Huns a rumor, and the bobwhites freeze out regularly. Every ringneck pheasant is a trophy to be savored. We're lucky to have them at all, and luckier still to hunt them in such a way that we pay our respects one bird at a time.

JOHN
BARSNESS

John Barsness was born and raised in Montana, where his grandparents homesteaded, and he shot his first game bird as soon as legally possible. With his wife, the writer Eileen Clarke, he now lives on a trout stream in an obscure part of the southwestern quarter of the state. He's never held a real job for a whole year, instead devoting his life to hunting, fishing, and gazing at long vistas.

In addition to writing for a number of national magazines, including Gray's Sporting Journal, Outdoor Life, Field & Stream, Sports Illustrated, *and* Sports Afield, *he's presently a contributing editor of* Peterson's Hunting. *His books include* Hunting the Great Plains, Montana Time: The Seasons of Trout Fisherman, *and* Western Skies: Bird Hunting on the High Plains and in the Rockies.

Though he has shot wild birds over a dozen breeds of pedigreed hunting dogs, a half-dozen accomplished mongrels, and dropped a francolin flushed by a baboon in Africa, his own dogs have been Labrador retrievers. He sees no reason to change and is working heartily toward an opinionated old age.

three

PHEASANTS WEST
OF THE 100TH

by John Barsness

Hunting pheasants to the left of that arbitrary definition of the West, the 100th meridian of longitude, is indeed different from hunting pheasants east of the line. For one, some of the country remains truly wild, and pilgrims still run into trouble along the fringes of the wilderness.

Fifteen autumns ago I was living in western Montana, about forty miles from the Idaho border, a country of flat-bottomed trout valleys surrounded by thickly timbered mountains. Though it doesn't look anything like the Midwest we think of as the center of the pheasant universe, it does resemble a more feral and vertical version of the Willamette Valley of western Oregon, where ring-necked pheasants first multiplied in North America.

That November a friend and I had been assigned the pleasant task of hunting down and shooting a few mallards and pheasants for the Thanksgiving table. We planned to hunt a ranch we knew at the base of the Mission Mountains. The Missions are as steep and craggy as the Tetons, but they don't have a national park surrounding them, just a wilderness area inside the mountains. Since you can't drive through them, even many natives remain unaware that the Missions hold all sorts of wild stuff, right next to the grain farms, trailer parks, and tourist traps of the Flathead Valley.

We drove up there two days before Thanksgiving and talked cows and weather with the rancher for a while. Then he mentioned the grizzlies. "You know they been hanging out around here," he said. We nodded. There had been a newspaper story about how the berry crop had failed in the mountains that summer. Bears from the Missions had followed the alder-lined creeks out into the valley, looking for food before their long winter's nap.

"A big sow and two cubs were right out there early one morning last week." He pointed across the gravel road to an alfalfa field. "Everybody's been taking their kids to meet the school bus ever since, sitting in the cars until the bus comes to make sure it's safe. We haven't seen any bears since then, but they're around. They just stick to the thick stuff during the day." He paused, looking west to where the field ended a half mile away. We could see the tops of cottonwoods and alders where the field dropped off into the creek bottom. "I wouldn't hunt the creek if I were you."

We thanked him, then walked across the road. We had both spent enough time among grizzlies not to discount what he said, but we also knew that grizzlies leave plenty of sign. They eat a lot of grass and berries and excrete a lot of leftovers. Plus, four-hundred-pound bears leave big tracks in soft, moist soil. We'd just keep an eye out around any thick cover.

This field was ideal for both roosters and mallards, the hay grown just enough since its last cutting in August to afford good pecking and grazing for the birds. Through the middle of the mile-long field ran a sinuous irrigation ditch, banks overgrown and a foot of water still flowing along the bottom. Pheasants liked to loaf in the wild roses along the banks, and mallards liked to rest in the bends of the ditch.

We split up, surrounding the big bend where we often found mallards. My partner circled to the right, crossing the ditch at an irrigation headgate, while I went left, my old black Lab Gillis at heel. When we were both a hundred yards from the bend, we moved in. The ducks were right where we expected to

find them, about a dozen, and mostly drakes. I shot two, one on my side of the ditch and one that fell in the water, and my friend killed another on his side. Gillis jumped in the ditch for the floater while we picked up the field birds.

We walked back down the ditch toward the creek, my friend looping ahead and standing while I worked Gillis through the roses along the banks. I killed one young rooster that held too tightly, and my friend killed an old bird that ran and then flushed out across the field, not quite far enough away from a load of 5s. So we were one pheasant short of Thanksgiving when we reached the edge of the creek.

It looked birdy, and when we walked down the slick grassy hill to the edge of the alders we couldn't find any sign of a bear. There were lots of deer tracks, however, and we took that to mean no grizzlies. So I sent Gillis in.

We heard him patter through the downed leaves under the alders, a quiet, anticipatory sound under the gray sky. And then something big jumped in the brush, alder branches cracking for three seconds, and I immediately thought deer, until we heard a low woof, much too deep and chesty for a seventy-pound dog. Gillis came loping out of the alders, hair ridged like the fin of a sailfish, looking back as he ran—so damn scared he was afraid to leave his rump unwatched. One experienced bear man from Alaska claims that even a rat terrier can chase a brown bear away. With salmon-mellowed coastal grizzlies, maybe so. It doesn't always work that way with hungrier mountain grizzlies.

So we backed up along the open base of the hill toward the road, shotguns halfway to our shoulders. Along the way we found where a big bear had walked across the moist creek bottom, could plainly see where the long claws had dug thimble-sized chunks of dirt in a rough line a couple of inches in front of the pad prints. Black bears don't leave those marks, even in soft soil. And so we made do with only five birds on Thanksgiving.

The next week two college students, new to the West and hunting without a dog, headed into the same creek's alders about a half mile upstream and surprised a grizzly in its day bed. They might have fared better if they hadn't tried to shoot the bear off with their pheasant guns. Then again, they might not have. One of the hunters spent most of a month in the hospital, and several experienced game wardens spent a very bad day tracking down the wounded grizzly and killing it. But no schoolchildren were eaten that fall, and soon the bears went back up into the mountains to den.

In the years since, I have assiduously avoided hunting anything in grizzly country except game that provides an excuse for carrying a .338, animals like mule deer and elk. But sending a dog into the thick stuff still startles both of us occasionally. I now live in the open, semidesert mountains along the upper reaches of the Missouri River. Where the river enters a big reservoir there's a public hunting area, full of cottonwoods and willows and alders, covering six square miles of the Missouri delta where it enters the lake. It's full of whitetails and pheasants—and other things.

One early December day two seasons ago I took my present Labrador, a much larger chocolate dog named Keith, down there for the year's last pheasant hunt. During the first hour he put up a few hen pheasants and even more deer, so I thought it was another deer when the alders crackled twenty yards in front of us. Then I thought it was somebody's stray horse until it stepped into a break in the alders and looked at me: a cow moose. Her spring calf stood up, on the other side of Keith, and we were suddenly standing between a mama moose and her five-hundred-pound darling. Something deep inside Keith told him it wouldn't be wise to make a false start at these deer—as he often did with whitetails, just to see them run. He stood still until I whistled softly. He trotted carefully back to heel and the two moose trotted carefully away.

Our pheasants live not only in grizzly and moose country, but out where the deer and the antelope play. I have hunted them in places where even jackrabbits barely make a comfortable living, where you can sit up on a hilltop and glass for pheasants as you would for mule deer. One of my favorite pheasant places is not exactly crawling with birds, but I like it because it so little resembles traditional pheasant cover that nobody else hunts it.

It lies along a "crick" in eastern Montana. What passes for a stream out there is usually the seasonal wash where spring snowmelt and summer rain drain into the Musselshell River. These cricks, however, have what pheasants always need, permanent water. During the fall they don't flow, instead seeping underground through sand and gravel left by the last glacier, welling up every few hundred yards in little pools. Like all desert ponds, these pools hold surprising numbers of wild things. Mice and voles and rabbits and other small mammals are attracted to the lusher vegetation around the shores, and in the water live Great Plains toads and leopard frogs and painted turtles and even a few small fish, mostly varieties of dace. Bull snakes often hunt the margins, and occasionally even prairie rattlers can be found, though for some reason I rarely run into Brother Rattlesnake unless I'm looking for him, which isn't often.

The pheasants run up and down the four miles of pools. I knew there were a few roosters around, but never tried hunting them specifically until one evening when I was sitting on a hillside, Keith beside me, glassing for sage grouse (a not uncommon method out here), when I saw two roosters skulking through the sagebrush. They were trotting up a dry coulee, just above one of the crick's pools, along the taller sage that grew along the bottom of the draw, just like a couple of sage birds except faster and more nervous.

So we made a big circle around the back side of their hill and worked down the draw. Halfway down Keith started acting birdy but nothing happened. Then I chanced to look into the crick bottom and saw both birds run right by the pool and up the opposite hill into the tall sage three hundred yards away. It was obvious that a man and a dog weren't going to surround those boys.

In the years since, I have figured out how to get an occasional shot at sagebrush pheasants. The inspiration came from Ben Burshia, the old Dakota-Assiniboine Indian I hunted with in northeastern Montana for most of a decade. That country more closely resembles the Midwest, but still possesses little enough water to qualify as western. One day we were out bird hunting, bouncing from one deep draw to another in Ben's pickup, when my bladder could stand it no longer and I told him to stop the damn truck. It was a little after noon and Ben didn't brake right away. Instead he drove down into the draw and parked next to one of the those prairie-crick pools surrounded by tall grass and cattails. I leapt out and while standing with my Levis unbuttoned next to the cattails could vaguely hear Ben clacking the action on his pumpgun. Ten seconds later the cattails in front of me began to move. Whatever was moving them headed for the water and I thought muskrat or maybe skunk until a big rooster climbed out of the cattails and then folded into the water when Ben's 20-gauge went off behind me and to the left.

I turned and looked at him. He was already tamping fresh tobacco into his pipe and lighting it. Around the smoke he said, "You'll always find pheasants around water in the middle of the day." Then he smiled slightly and shrugged, as if there was nothing to it: water and noon equals rooster.

So that's how I hunt the dry cricks now, not waiting for the cool of December but instead hunting the warm days of late October. It is very pleasant, with no reason to get up particularly early, to lie in bed until absolutely awake on some sunny October morning, then have a leisurely breakfast (none of that in-the-dark burnt-toast duck-hunter stuff), and drive across the high plains. The distant islands of the Snowies or Bear Paws or Bighorns will already have that dead-level cap of first snow, as if their ridgelines rise into an invisible Arctic floating in the thin cirrus clouds; and the sagebrush will have a yellow tinge, the remains of the late-summer bloom, almost matching the breast feathers of the last male meadowlarks resting in the elastic branches of rabbit brush and sage. On the farthest ridge between you and the pale mountains, on the upper edge of the olive-yellow sea, six points as white as the mountain snow turn and run across the ridge—six pronghorns not trusting any pickup truck, no matter how distant, with opening day such a recent memory.

If you have chosen the day perfectly it will occur in that peculiar balanced week we call Indian summer, with the heat and dust of summer held pinned lightly to the earth by the first frosts. You can still smell the dust, an underlying scent like fresh-rinsed soap, but it doesn't dry the nostrils and the air shimmers absolutely clear above the sage, as if filtered through the yellow flowers themselves. The dog snorts under the sagebrush like a vacuum cleaner with circulatory problems, as if the autumnal equinox has cleaned out his sinuses and made the high plains the bird-dog equivalent of a Fellini movie—strange and yet so compelling you have to stick your nose in it and snort.

Along the crick there are a few cottonwoods, spindly things with a few yellow leaves still clinging, as sparse as the remnants of roast pheasant breast caught between the teeth. But you know that just to the left of the largest cottonwood, the lone tree with the golden eagle on the dead side-branch, there's a pool surrounded by jointgrass and a patch of wild roses. And there a pheasant might live.

The trick here is to approach the unseen pool like you would a sleeping deer, as cautiously as possible from downwind, because even though pheasants can't smell worth a hoot (thank God) they can hear like feathered bats. You have learned in past hunts that the pool lies in a deep hole, dammed by a slanted crumbling shale shelf full of trilobites and other unfortunate Ordovicians. Below the shale the dry crick twists through the sage again.

Since the pool lies spang in the middle of the buffalo plains, the only way to hunt it is to circle widely, waddling bent-over up the crick like a duck, the dog at heel, then run to the top of the angled shale and pin the birds in the cover along the banks. Otherwise all you're likely to produce is the unsatisfactory memory of roosters running a quarter mile away through the sage, tailfeathers near-erect like pointy middle digits, sending you their regards.

You have to hiss at the dog three or four times during the last hundred yards: he's finding traces of that morning's scent in the compacted sand along the wash's bottom. But he heels, wound tight enough that when you make the last run up the shale and then slam to a halt (like a crooked Statue of Liberty with a shotgun instead of a torch), he's already galumphing toward the wild roses and jointgrass. The first bird comes up mottled tan, a hen, but the second has a tail so long that the longest feather is bent by twisting through the short rosebush tunnels. The faraway bead on the full-choke barrel slides along the broken feather, the hard-flying body, and then past that squawking head and kapow! there are feathers all over the sagebrush. Another rooster gets up at the upper end of the roses, flying directly away, and you put the bead up his tailfeathers and shoot. Feathers fly but he doesn't slow so you shoot again, biting your lip in the effort to drive an ounce-and-a-half of 4s up through the belly to the heart. Still flapping, he sinks into the sage like a fighter plane that never quite got enough speed off the deck of a carrier, and the dog runs past the first dead rooster, disappearing into the tall sage after the cripple. In ten seconds you see his square brown head rise with a big loose bird in his mouth, the long tail flipping toward the sky each time the dog readjusts his tooth-grip on the breast feathers, tailfeathers not so erect and defiant now. You feel pretty sly as you take the first bird and send the dog back for the second, but by the time both are in the game vest and you're headed back across the olive sea you are caught in that odd reversal of the plains: suddenly you're too small under that huge curve of sky, as if the universe is always behind you, like Paul Bunyan's Hide-Behind. No matter which way you turn the cirrus sky will turn with you and some part of this wide-open world will escape. Even if you legally possess the two birds you killed and took from the sky, you will never possess one millionth of the plains, even in memory.

There have been many western pheasant places like that: the badlands on the south side of the Missouri over in North Dakota; the tablelands on top covered with fields of durum wheat, the table dropping off into hard-bitten draws full of thorny buffalo-berry. The roosters came up almost vertically from the berry patches; the trick was to bring the shotgun up from below and shoot as the bead touched their heads. Or the slough of the Yellowstone, ten-foot cattails on the lowland side and irrigated barley on the other. The pheasants would fly from the cattails in mid-afternoon to feed on the barley, then digest and dust for an hour or so in the wild roses along the shore before flying back to their beloved cattails, where they were as unhuntable as Cape buffalo in elephant grass. Or the alder-swamp pheasants along the Judith River, where you needed hip boots to wallow around the edges of beaver ponds, shooting the birds just as you would ruffed grouse except, of course, pressing your lips hard at each shot, willing those birds dead on contact, because otherwise they might drift under a beaver dam where nothing less than a backhoe could retrieve them. Or the December snow along the Poplar where you and the dog followed the pheasant tracks into the shoulder-high rosebushes, pushing the herd of birds ahead of you along the deer trails to the edge of the river. You'd both stand there with breath hanging in the air, gray alders and cottonwoods along the bank above the slush-ice river, until the birds lost their nerve, trapped between you and the water. First a hen, then two, and then finally a rooster would spray out of the snow and fall to the quick shot of the old 12-gauge double gun.

Those are the western pheasant places I remember best, even though there have been better places to hunt them—

"better" meaning more birds, in more conventional stretches of farmland cover. Still there are quite a few of those places, looking exactly like transplanted chunks of Iowa scattered among the mountains and out on the arid plains. Even a decade ago they were largely hunted only by locals. There might have been some difficulty getting permission if those pieces of micro-Midwest were next to a "big" town of eight thousand or more—places where only parish priests and family doctors got to hunt—but if you knocked on enough doors, far enough away from anything resembling a city, you could get on, as they say out here.

But then something happened. Actually, it has always— will always happen, unless plagues and wars kill enough of us to leave room on earth for the rest of what lives here. Forty years ago there used to be wonderful places to hunt wild pheasants east of the Mississippi, but now we have filled them up with subdivisions full of quaint homes, shopping malls full of stores that sell almost anything that isn't needed to exist, and new factories that make all the stuff we buy in the shopping malls to put in our homes. In between are eight-lane highways, so we can drive from the homes to the malls to the factories. All of these are filled with one hundred million new Americans, added in those forty years.

In between are the shrinking places where birds and other wild things live. We keep dumping new and improved chemicals into these, to produce more food in less space for the one hundred million new Americans. Then we express surprise and outrage when pheasants disappear. We pack up and head where the air is cleaner and highways mostly have two lanes. Where wild birds can still live.

Word gets out: there's wonderful pheasant hunting still to be had in North Dakota or Montana or eastern Washington. This past October my wife and I happened to be driving along one of the loneliest highways in the Lower 48, through the middle of the sagebrush sea, where I once drove over one hundred miles and met two other vehicles.

One of those dry "cricks" parallels the highway for about thirty miles. It happened to be opening day of pheasant season, a date I often forget because opening days tend to be crowded, even in the West. And every quarter to half mile along the barbwire fence separating the highway from the crick was parked a vehicle with a dog box. Often there were two or three vehicles clumped together. Off along the dull purple willow brush of every bend in the crick were hunters wearing orange bird vests. It reminded me of a weekend I once spent during deer season in Pennsylvania.

What it comes down to is that there are no secret places left to hunt wild pheasants. You can come out here and visit—or even live—and it will be different than it is now back east, or in California. You will be hunting wild birds instead of paying for pen-raised roosters. But the frontier is gone. Just as the buffalo suddenly disappeared (sixty million to less than a thousand) within a decade in the late nineteenth century, the wide-open bird hunting has disappeared in less than a decade of the late twentieth century. You may be able to buy some of it, or rent it from a rancher or outfitter, but the days of people expressing amazement that anyone would travel all that way, just to hunt a mere bird, are gone. The secret places have all been found.

We can point fingers in all sorts of directions. I can point at least two or three at myself. We all love to tell secrets, but mere secret-telling isn't what spreads Americans inexorably across America.

We keep using it up. We have since the first Americans crossed the Bering land bridge and started knocking giant sloths in the head, since Columbus sailed the ocean blue and Pilgrims pushed the Indians out of Plymouth Bay. This started the domino effect that pushed the Sioux out of Minnesota and then out of the Black Hills and got Custer killed. Lately the same domino effect pushed eastern urbanites to the suburbs, and then to California, and then to Colorado. Right now the first signs of urban hunting have begun here in Montana: the valley where I grew up now supports three shooting "preserves" where you pay to hunt pen-raised pheasants. This has happened because the valley has been half subdivided, and even where pheasants still find a brushy crick to live along, sixteen screenwriters, hairdressers, and trust-funders own the brush—not one rancher. And none of them want you shooting pheasants in their twenty-acre back yard.

Which is why quite often on summer nights I lie awake and listen to the coyotes singing on the ridge and find myself wondering if the chokecherry patch between the house and the crick will have cherries this year. The cherries attract pheasants and Hungarian partridge, and even a few porcupines and ruffed grouse. I lie awake not so much worrying about the chokecherry crop, because like rain and drought it has always come and gone, and the wild world just keeps truckin'. I lie awake like a grizzly bear, hearing voices from outside the edges of the wild, saying there's no place for grizzly bears, that the world would be a better place if we didn't have to worry about grizzly bears eating our kids while they wait for the school bus, or beating us up when we're hunting pheasants. And something in the coyotes' voices tells me that when the grizzlies go, wild pheasants won't be far behind.

ROBERT F. JONES

Robert F. Jones was for many years a senior writer at Time *and* Sports Illustrated. *His essays and short stories have appeared in fifteen previous anthologies and a host of magazines, including* Audubon, Gray's Sporting Journal, *and* Fly Rod & Reel. *He writes a bird-hunting column, "The Dawn Patrol," for* Shooting Sportsman.

Born in Wisconsin, where he learned his love of the outdoors, Jones has since hunted and fished on every continenet but Antarctica. The author of five novels and four works of nonfiction, including the award-winning Upland Passage: A Field Dog's Education, *and* Jake: A Labrador Puppy at Work & Play *(Farrar, Straus & Giroux, 1992), Jones recently completed a sixth novel,* Tie My Bones to Her Back, *set on the Great Plains in the 1870s. A collection of his big game stories,* African Twilight, *was published last fall.*

four

GLORIOUS CARNAGE

by Robert F. Jones

he sad thing about living through a golden age is that you don't appreciate it while it's happening. The label is only applied later, when whatever art or craft or wonder the age apotheosizes has turned to lead.

By all accounts, the heyday of pheasant hunting in North America took place during the decade right after World War II, when I was in my teens. The birds had been thriving in the heart of the continent since the early twentieth century, enjoying the largesse of that great but already doomed American institution, the family farm. With its woodlots and weedy edges, its corn and grain fields, its fallow ground grown tall in native grasses and seed-bearing forbs, its swamps and marshes and low soggy places as yet undrained and thus still unplowed, the family farm was approximately pheasant heaven. There the long-tailed birds could feed heartily, roost quietly, hide from their natural enemies when danger threatened, and raise their broods in relative peace. Egg-weakening pesticides were not yet in widespread use, and harvesting techniques were cruder than they are today, so that enough corn, wheat, barley, or rye was left on the ground after the combines went through for plenty of birds to survive even the harshest of winters.

The war itself had given pheasant populations a boost. The younger men who normally hunted them hardest each fall were off somewhere in military service. Gas and tire rationing and the scarcity of shotgun shells kept all but the keenest of the remaining gunners out of the pheasant fields and cast a cloak of peace over the midwestern countryside. In 1945, the pheasant population of North and South Dakota alone was close to 30 million. Today the whole U.S. probably contains no more than that number of the birds.

I started hunting during that prelapsarian age of abundance, but of course I was unaware of the unique opportunities it offered. Growing up in southern Wisconsin, I was not all that far —maybe six hundred miles, at best twelve hours nonstop by car on the slow roads of those two-lane blacktop days—from the epicenter of the pheasant quake: Sioux Falls, South Dakota. As soon as I was old enough to drive, I should have begged, borrowed, or hot-wired a car, bade sayonara to my kinfolk, and headed west to the Dakotas with naught but my dog and gun. Yet I only went there once to hunt. A classmate and hunting buddy of mine was the son of a wealthy businessman who had standing invitations to hunt the big spreads northwest of Sioux Falls every fall, and in 1948 Jack and I went with him.

It was my first trip away from home without my parents, and there must have been a thousand heady new sights, sounds, smells, and ideas that impressed me as much as the hunting itself. But now all that remains in my fading memory are *the clouds...*

Yes, that's just what they were—whole cloud banks of birds getting up from the corn rows after each drive, getting up all at once with a hell of a racket, a rattling, cackling, metallic rush of sound, a tornadic roar compounded as much of primary feathers thrashing against dry cornstalks as it was of irate birds screaming; big explosions of color separating and lifting like giant flakes from the yellow-green background of standing corn—bronze-red-green-white-dun-colored splashes enclosed in swirls of wing-fanned dust—and over it all the thump of big-bore shotguns, ragged at first but blending finally into a steady crescendo.

The same sounds came from cornfields all around us, as far as the ear could hear. I remember thinking later that this was what the Civil War must have sounded like during big battles—Chickamauga or Chancellorsville or Gettysburg—sporadic firing at first as the skirmish lines met and felt each other out, then halfhearted volleys while platoons came into the line, then the whole thing rising in intensity at last to a sustained drumroll of musketry. All that was lacking were the cannons—though some of those 10-gauge magnums banged nearly as loud.

The battlefield metaphor applied as well to the most effective hunting technique employed in those days of abundance: The Drive. We hunted big fields, five or ten acres each of standing corn, maybe more. A couple of dozen men and boys would take part in these drives—half as "pushers" or drivers, the other half as blockers, who got most of the shooting. The drives usually took place in midmorning or late afternoon, when the pheasants were busy feeding. Dogs were rarely used in these drives, though I recall that exceptions were made for a few well-trained Labradors and springers who could be trusted to stay coolly at heel until the shooting stopped. A whining or barking dog could ruin a drive early on by causing the alerted pheasants to leak out around the edges of the drive line before flushing. Any pheasant, wild-born or pen-raised, would rather run than fly.

While the blockers quietly took their positions at the bottom of the field, the pushers mustered at the far end, forming a shallow, cup-shaped line of men stationed no more than ten yards apart. Any wider a dispersal would allow birds to sneak back between the pushers. You wouldn't think so gaudy a creature as the ringneck—a bird, moreover, that weighs three pounds and measures three feet from beak to tailtip—could get so invisible so quickly. But they could. At a signal from the drive-master's police whistle, the pushers started forward. They had to march at a slow, steady, almost military pace—no straggling or sprinting ahead permitted—to keep the line intact and properly dressed.

They zigzagged slightly as they marched, covering as much ground as possible. Because pushing was less likely than blocking to produce lots of good fast shooting, most of the pushers were boys or young men. The rich old guys with their beer bellies got to block. Jack and I did a lot of pushing that week.

Gun safety was always on everyone's mind. The local newspapers and radio stations wouldn't let you forget it: "Teen Killed on Fatal Pheasant Drive," "Fargo Resident Blinded by Shotgun Blast." Here you had two rows of armed men, one approaching the other at a slow walk. Nerves on both sides were screwed to the yelping point, as if in impending battle. When the birds started to panic, to run and then to fly, the temptation would be strong—almost overpowering—to shoot straight ahead, and to shoot far too low. No one wanted to collect a face full of No. 5s at close range. Nor to be the one who delivered it. The rules were clear and firmly enforced: Shoot only at high birds, no hens, and preferably only after they'd passed you, going away.

Here's what I recall of a typical drive near Slodeth, South Dakota, nearly half a century ago. A crisp, clear October morning, temperature in the low fifties, sky the blue of Betty Grable's peepers. The hollow banging of gunfire drums in the distance, all around us. Hendry Gobel, who owns the farmland we're hunting, stands in the middle of the drive line. He's a tall, fat, ruddy-cheeked farmboy-cum-entrepreneur in his early thirties, a decorated infantry veteran of WWII in Europe, now a big wheel in the chamber of commerce who doubles as the town's Chevy dealer and owns the local feed store as well. Wearing a flap-eared Elmer Fudd hunting cap and a red-and-black-checked deer-hunting coat over his Oshkosh-B'gosh bib overalls, knee-high lace-up leather boots caked with Dakota mud and cow dung, he totes a scarred but well-oiled Winchester Model 12, its 30-inch barrel extended with a bulbous Poly-Choke. Hendry Gobel talks with a Dutchy lilt. "Okey-dokey, poys, dere's lotza dem longtails in dis field today—see 'em in dere, down between da rows? When I plo da vissel, you guys *marsch!*"

"Jawohl, Herr Obersturmbahnführer," Jack mutters beside me. Yes, Hendry Gobel is a wee bit bossy.

But Hendry was right: we *could* see the pheasants down there between the rows, dozens at least, perhaps as many as a hundred of them, stalking jerkily, chickenlike, pecking at windfallen corncobs, the long-spurred cocks strutting in their gorgeous vanity while the drab hens scuttled humbly around their lords and masters. Nervously I shifted my gun, a well-worn old 12-gauge Winchester Model 97 pump that Jack's dad had loaned me for this hunt. It was his old gun. He was now shooting a Belgian Browning. My own single-shot 28-gauge wasn't quite the ticket for these birds and I'd left it back home in Wisconsin. Most of the guys I knew shot long-barrelled, unplugged autoloaders or pumps on pheasants in those days. You rarely saw a double gun in the fields where the longtails played. My loaner was choked modified, but most of the others wore Poly-Chokes. The bulges on the ends of the barrels made them look like tank cannons. Blockers set their Poly-Chokes at open-cylinder, very effective at close range, while pushers preferred modified or even improved-modified settings for the longer shots they were likely to get. Some of the better or at least more confident shots even set them at full.

A sharp blast from Hendry Gobel's whistle set us in motion. I could see a few pheasants look up at the harsh sound— the cocks with their feathery blue "ears" atip—and begin scuttling toward the end of the field. We walked steadily, our weapons at port arms, gun butts thwacking the dry cornstalks, Hendry muttering occasional orders to slow down or speed up or to keep our intervals neat and tidy. I could see sunlight glinting off the gunbarrels of the blockers. About halfway down the field a rooster panicked and flew, left to right. Hendry Gobel upped on the bird and dropped it as it cleared the right side of the field—a fifty-yard shot, maybe sixty. He was one of the more confident shooters.

At Hendry's shot, other birds got up and some flew toward the blocking line. The shooting began, ragged at first, then faster.

"*Schnell!*" Hendry yelled. "Move faster, poys! Ve gotta get 'em up right now!"

We dogtrotted down the corn rows, our blood up, whooping and yelling like the Iron Brigade at Antietam, slapping the dry corn with our free hands, and the birds flushed almost in unison. The gunfire sounded like nonstop thunder and suddenly it was raining pheasants. A cock came cackling right toward me, the ripped-metal blare getting louder with each beat of his wings. I skidded to a halt and swung with him as he swept past me, seeing his bright black eye locked on mine, then took him going away in a flurry of tiny rump feathers. Another came blowing past me and I swung and hit the trigger. Nothing. I'd forgotten to work the slide. By the time I shucked in another shell, most of the birds were dead or gone. All across the bottom of the field, feathers filtered down through the still morning air. But then as we walked the remaining distance toward the blockers a single skulking rooster flushed from beneath my feet—straight up. I nailed him at the top of his rise just an instant before Jack shot. When that once-beauteous bird hit the ground it was nothing but rags.

"I guess it's yours," Jack said.

"What's left of him," I said. "Thanks for nothing."

I think we bagged more than fifty cock pheasants on that drive alone—the number that sticks in my fading memory is fifty-six. Of course I'd killed only two of them, and Jack had three, plus his spoiling shot on my last bird. Hendry Gobel dropped five, one for each round in his gun, as did some of the other more experienced shooters, Jack's dad among them. It was slaughter, no doubt about it, but what the hell, why not? The birds were there in abundance—no, in *over*abundance. In a way they were a cash crop. The more of them we killed, the less corn they'd eat from Hendry Gobel's fields, and thus the more money he'd realize from his harvest. Not only that, but Hendry charged the guests who stayed in his big, roomy farmhouse fifteen dollars a day for the privilege, which included delicious meals heavy on roast pheasant stuffed with apples and sauerkraut.

But the drives, though exciting and highly productive, weren't near as much fun as the hunts Jack and I made alone during the early afternoons. While the old guys swilled schnapps and beer, played sheepshead, or took their sonorous siestas, Jack and I worked the edges of Gobel's swamp land down near Tomahawk Slough for nooning roosters. Hendry's young black Lab, Mädchen, was only too glad to accompany us. In hip boots and high spirits we slogged the marshes with Maddy porpoising ahead. It was fast, awkward shooting when she flushed a bird, standing ankle deep in the muck, unable to shift our feet quickly, snap-shooting usually at big fast-jumping cock birds glimpsed only briefly through cattails and saw grass against the hard blue sky. Sometimes we fell, knocked backwards from the greasy grass hummocks by the recoil of off-balance shots, but the water always felt good in that heat. I once emerged from a dunking with a mud turtle in my boot. We usually dragged back to the farmhouse before three o'clock, sweaty, flushed, reeking of foul-smelling swamp slime—but carrying at least half a dozen roosters between us. Gobel would tut-tut at our filth, grin fondly at our birds, sluice off the worst of the muck with a garden hose, and then it was off for another field drive…

So that was my moment in pheasant heaven. I never thought I'd see its like again. But I was wrong, though it took awhile.

Soon after the South Dakota excursion I discovered girls. Then it was college, followed by a stint in the Navy, marriage, fatherhood, a newspaper job in Milwaukee, then a move to New York and later Los Angeles for *Time* magazine. Then back to New York again for the psychedelic sixties—the Vietnam War, the counterculture, assassinations, riots in the black ghettos, and suchlike follies.

Not much time for hunting with all that going on. But I finally got back to it on a serious basis in 1964, when my wife and I bought a house in northernmost Westchester County, about an hour by commuter train from New York City. Behind the house lay nine hundred acres of hilly, undeveloped woodland and overgrown hayfields. It was prime cover for grouse and woodcock back then—alder brakes down low for the bogsuckers, lots of ancient but still-fruitful apple trees, plenty of white pines for grouse to roost in, wild cherries, fox-grape hells, hickories, and big stands of sumac and doghair aspen up high, the whole of it crisscrossed with miles of neatly built stone walls along which the pats liked to skulk. But there were always a few pheasants hanging out in the uncut meadows that dotted the second-growth woods. I soon had a canine team to help me harass them—a big yellow Lab named Simba and a keen but slightly wacky German shorthair called Max.

These pheasants were the wild descendants of stock initially released before World War II, not pen-raised birds. They were fast afoot, veritable Roger Bannisters of roosterdom, and extremely reluctant to fly even when pinned dead to rights by the pointer. But Simba quickly learned that whenever Max locked up, his best bet was to circle out beyond the bird, then move back in on it. We got our share of flushes. I still remember one longtail that almost eluded us. It was a snowy day in November. We'd hunted the long wooded ridge at the top of a big meadow, then struck off down the brush-grown stone wall that bisected the field. From the way the dogs acted I knew there was a pheasant running ahead of them. Simba finally got ahead of it near the bottom and the bird flushed—a rooster. But before I could mount the gun it had lighted in the uppermost branches of a tall ash tree, from which lofty vantage point it looked down and gave us the raspberry in the form of a jeering, cocksure cackle.

What to do? I'd gotten religion by then and refused on principle to pot the bird out of the tree. We waited it out—five minutes, ten minutes—hoping he'd get nervous and fly. He didn't. Finally I leaned my gun within easy reach against the ash trunk, made a snowball and threw it at the pheasant. But I'm no Warren Spahn. I zinged half a dozen snowballs at that cock bird before I threw a strike. He whirled and launched; I grabbed the gun, fumbled at the safety—and missed him twice. He soared back up the way we'd come down, finally landing at the top of the field a quarter mile away.

The dogs seemed amused at my bad marksmanship. "All right, lads," I told them gruffly, "let's start hiking." We plodded back uphill through the ankle-deep snow, halting near where I'd marked the rooster down. Up there, thanks to the wind, the snow lay thinner on the ground. The field had been mowed in the late summer and the grass was short, just the tips of it showing through the fluffy white cover. Any gaudy cock bird hunkered down in that stubble would have stood out like a zit on a teenager's face. No bird in sight. But then I noticed a straight line of taller grass, about a foot high, that grew along a fallen strand of wire, the remnants of an electric fence long out of use. I started walking the wire with the dogs just ahead of me. About halfway along, the snow suddenly erupted as the rooster took flight—from a patch of grass you wouldn't think could hide a field mouse.

I rolled him twenty yards out…

That's the way it was with those pheasants of the near northeast. I pretty much despaired of ever again seeing the kind of nonstop, slam-bang pheasant shooting I'd enjoyed in the heartland as a boy. Meanwhile, burnt out on global violence, I had quit *Time* magazine and joined up with *Sports Illustrated,* where I covered the gentler worlds of pro football, motor sports, and the outdoors. One of my beats was the Formula I racing circuit, and in 1973 at the U.S. Grand Prix in Watkins Glen, New York, I met Lord Alexander Hesketh. Then twenty-three years old, he was a plump, witty, wealthy, and somewhat flaky Brit who had entered a new F-I team into the lists. His driver was the late James Hunt, a handsome, nervy young stalwart who went on to win the World Driving Championship but achieved greater name recognition when the actor Richard Burton stole his wife. Over dinner one night in Corning, New York, Alexander was telling me about his baronial estate, Easton Neston, north of London. "We've got loads of pheasants," His Lordship said. "Why don't you pop over some time for a shoot?"

I pounced on the invitation like a springer on a covey of quail.

In January of 1974, the last month of the English pheasant season, I flew to London and then headed north, roughly a two hour's drive from Piccadilly Circus. Easton Neston stands on seven thousand acres near the town of Towcester (sounds like "toaster"). The Hesketh manor house, built largely of marble, was begun in the late 1680s and completed half a century later. The ceilings in some of its rooms were thirty feet tall. You could park a Rolls-Royce in any of the downstairs fireplaces, and maybe Alexander had; he was surely capable of it. Entering the house, I was first impressed by the sepulchral chill, then by the sight of a full-mounted brown bear rearing up in a dark hallway corner. Wintry light glinted off suits of armor arrayed behind the bear. On the table in the entry hall lay a paperback copy of *M.A.S.H. Goes to Maine*, a huge Bowie knife, and a guest book full of the scrawled signatures of Churchills, Windsors, and Douglas-Homes. In the echoing dining room, a brace of Rubens paintings added a touch of warmth to the background behind the butler's eyes. The erect figure of a stuffed snowy owl glowered from one corner. I stood near the crackling fireplace, warming my bum as I sipped a welcoming glass of sherry, and admired the tapestries on the walls. Beyond the mullions of the rain-streaked casement windows I could see pheasants strutting haughtily on the putting-green lawns. I was a long way from Hendry Gobel's farmhouse in South Dakota.

At dinner that evening the rest of the guests assembled, and after a few minutes it became evident that what we Americans take for satirical novels of English country life are nothing more than straight reportage. Consider if you will the Lambton sisters, Anne and Rose. Anne was a small, pale thing with the sharp-toothed grin of a dolphin. She affected a freaky air and a cockney accent—"wiv" for "with," and so forth—and feigned a total incomprehension of affairs in the "real world."

"Are vey still hafing vose 'orrible bombs in Londing?" she asked. "Oy 'aven't bean vare in mumfs. Oh pigs! Oy spilt me caviar!" She laughed with an oinking snort.

Her sister Rose was taller but even more out of touch, very pale with dyed dark-red hair. She'd brought her pet dog along, a tetchy little shelty bitch who lurked beneath the dining table nipping at ankles and whining now and then like a household ghost. Next to Rose sat Andrew Fraser, a younger son of Lord Lovat who led the No. 4 Commandos during World War II. A keen shot, dark, trim, and amused, Andrew seemed very fit—except for his right eye, which he'd damaged quite severely not long before when he threw a firecracker into a bonfire. "The surgeons removed the lens," he explained, very cool and dispassionate, "but the rest of the eye is still sound. They say that perhaps I can wear a contact lens and regain part of the sight, but until then I'm afraid my shooting is a bit off form."

Across from Fraser sat Robert Fermor-Hesketh, Alexander's younger brother. (A third brother, John, the youngest, was not present. An even keener shot than Fraser, he usually spends the bird season, from the Glorious 12th of August to the end of January, traveling around Britain in a car complete with a built-in bed, shooting partridge, pheasant, grouse, woodcock, and wildfowl wherever he can glean an invitation.) Robert Hesketh, or

"Bobs" as he's known, was a shorter, trimmer version of Alexander, who in those days stood at least six-foot-four and weighed 240. Wide-shouldered and flat-bellied by contrast, Bobs sported a leonine mane and bearing. Tough, bouncy, and glowering, he too was a crack shot and competitor, as would be evidenced the next morning under the flighted pheasants of Easton Neston.

Dawn broke through a fine, cold rain—little more than a mist, but with teeth in it. I'd debated long and hard over dressing for the shoot in English style—Wellies, moleskin breeks, Norfolk jacket, ascot, Barbour coat, oiled cotton shooting cap, maybe even one of those classy fold-down shooting sticks. But no, I couldn't go that route—too phony, too foppish. Instead I dressed in my usual upland attire: scuffed but well-greased Russell boots, khaki canvas brush pants and game jacket, worn over a red-checked wool shirt, and topped off with a scruffy Jones cap replete with the requisite grouse tailfeather. Let them sneer their limey sneers at the countrybred cousin from over the pond. I was a descendant of Natty Bumppo, by Gawd, and I'd shoot their eyes out...

Like hell I would.

We were eight guns that day, each man backed up by a loader to keep his matched pair of doubles primed and ready. My guns were slim, elegant, sidelocked Bosses, long-barreled 12-bores of course, courtesy of His Lordship (though only for the day, alas). My loader was a short, cheery assistant gamekeeper named Sid Watker, who chattered merrily as we slogged though a field of winter wheat to the first stand of the day.

"Ah, yes," quoth Sid, "most of the land is under cultivation, but His Lordship maintains about seven thousand pheasant on the estate, that he does, and shoots it only six or eight times a season, killing up to eight hundred birds a go. But today I reckon we won't kill no more than five or six hundred, not with the weather like this—watch your step there, sir, it's mucky goin', innit?—no, this rain will keep 'em from flyin', too heavy they get in the wet like this, they'd rather run than fly,"—and where had I heard that before?—"but here come the beaters now, sir, you'd better get ready."

The beaters, some fifty men and boys and a few small girls from the neighboring village, pushed through the first patch of wood, trilling and chirruping and bellowing to frighten the pheasants ahead of them, thwacking the bushes and tree trunks with their clubs, now and then coshing a hare or rabbit as it tried to cut back through the line. The gamekeeper, a red-faced sergeant-major type who ran the shoot with an iron hand, directed the beaters with his police whistle (just like Hendry Gobel) and I was reminded once again that there is as much discipline and tactical skill involved in this type of shooting as there is in a company-scale infantry maneuver.

As the beaters neared the wood edge we could see the pheasants milling—tall, tan, scuttling figures—reluctant to approach the open ground. Then they exploded with a rattle of wet wings and lined out toward the guns where we stood a hundred yards away in the open field, each man fifty yards from his nearest neighbor. By the time the birds reached us, they were at full flight speed and thirty yards high.

Guns began slamming all up and down the line. Blue smoke hung suspended in the drizzle and drifted slowly in the light cold air. The birds, when hit, seemed to double in size, their feathers puffing, then crumpling and falling with wings all askew. They thumped hard on the wet ground. Then again that strange phenomenon, only witnessed when clouds of birds are killed directly overhead. What appeared to be bronze snowflakes began to fall from the sky: pheasant feathers. Soon they were thick as a blizzard. I caught a glimpse, between shots, of James Hunt poking awkwardly at a high double, missing both birds. He had never shot before.

I saw Andrew Fraser, bad eye and all, center a cock bird, then with his left barrel, knock feathers from another which sloped away to fall behind the shooting line. Not to worry, the dogs—thick-bodied, keen-eyed Labs who waited phlegmatically to the rear—would gather him up later with the other wounded birds. I watched Robert Hesketh just long enough to see him drop five doubles in a row, faster than it takes to write this sentence, all the birds falling within ten yards of where he stood. None of them thrashed for even a moment. As for me, on that first drive, I killed some birds, but wounded or missed a lot more.

While the dogs collected the dead and the cripples, we guns moved to the next drive, a gloomy spot known as "The Wilderness." My post was at the edge of the wood, in a cut among some pines. The birds came out of the trees fast and low, appearing in full flight only ten yards from me as they bored through the feathery upper branches. It was snap shooting of the sort familiar to North American grouse and woodcock shooters, and my score quickly improved. I knocked down a clean double, then another, then a string of singles, mixed in with a few fretful misses, then a final double. Already my shoulder was aching. The Bosses, beautiful as they looked, were clearly too short for my length of pull.

Then a figure emerged from the stiffening rain. It was Alexander's mother, Kisty, the widow lady of the manor, a strong, handsome, friendly woman with a liking for America and Americans. Except for bright red knee socks, she was clad all in black— black breeks, black jacket, a wide-brimmed Andalusian-style hat, and a black eyepatch. She'd lost the sight of one eye as the result of a recent car crash, but the eyepatch gave her a jolly piratical look. Her good eye twinkled through the mist.

"I've been watching you, Yank," she said. "You shot well in this close cover. How do you like it so far?"

"Glorious carnage," I said.

She laughed. "Strange people, the English," she mused, knocking gobbets of clay from her boots with a gnarled walking stick. The mud fell with a sodden thump on a dead cock pheasant which lay at her feet. "They call this recreation."

The rest of the day was a blur of falling birds, my ears ringing with the hollow, ragged rage of 12-bore explosions, the hallooing of the beaters, the strident chirp of the gamekeeper's whistle. The whole world—black, gray, brown, green—smelled of blood and burned gunpowder. At one point, a pure white pheasant flushed and swiveled its way through the barrage, miraculously escaping unhit. At another, a small, shaggy animal that resembled a long-legged pig emerged from the woods, did a double-take on seeing the guns, and bounded back to safety. "Chinese barking deer," explained Kisty, who was strolling past at the moment. "A few of them wandered in here from an estate farther south. Ugly little things though, aren't they? We don't shoot 'em."

The final tally for the day was 580 pheasant, sixteen duck (mallards that flushed from ponds in the fields), a dozen woodcock, and eight wood pigeons. Only a middling score for Easton Neston. The gamekeepers laid the birds out for us near the manor house, on the putting-green lawn. It was quite a sight. I asked Sid Atker if he'd kept count on how many I'd shot.

"You did right well for a newcomer, sir," he said. "I counted seventy-eight pheasant that fell to your gun, plus a couple of woodcock and a pigeon or two. Right well indeed, I'd say."

Later, back in my room for a welcome, blood-warming bath, I noticed that my shooting arm was black and blue from shoulder to elbow, the inevitable legacy of ill-fitting guns. But it was a small price to pay for the experience. Once again I'd seen clouds of birds, and the heavens had blessed me with a snowfall of feathers. No, we hadn't done as well as the shooting party at Lord Stamford's park, which over four days in early January of 1864 had tallied 4,045 pheasants, 3,902 rabbits, 860 hares, and 59 woodcock. Nor would I personally pose much of a threat to the shooting record of the late Lord Ripon, who between 1867 and 1904 settled the hash of 142,343 pheasants, 97,759 partridge, 56,460 grouse, 29,858 rabbits, and 27,686 hares. Frankly, I doubt that anyone will. Yet I'm glad that I had at least two chances in my lifetime—in the South Dakota of 1948 and the English countryside of 1974—to see and shoot at masses of wild pheasants, veritable clouds of them.

It was glorious carnage indeed.

GENE HILL

Gene Hill, an associate editor of Field & Stream, *is the author of eight books of essays on the out-of-doors. Prior to being with* Field & Stream *he was the executive editor of* Sports Afield *and a vice president, creative director of J. Walter Thompson. He has trained and field trialed better-than-decent Labrador retrievers and a couple of middling English setters. He has hunted birds and big game in a long list of places and is an eager, if not notable, clay target shooter. Fly fishing takes up what time is left, especially in tarpon and bonefish water, unless there is a chance for Atlantic salmon.*

five

Ten-Second Pheasants

by Gene Hill

It was only a small stream with an edging of marsh, no more than eight to ten feet across. But it was spongy and we poked around for a dry crossing while the Labs thrashed through the creek washing off the prairie dust and ignoring any attempt to bring them under control. We finally just waded over, wet only to the knees, and in a minute the water was forgotten.

I saw a covered wagon, dangling with chicken coops, buckets, coils of rope, and what have you. A small family, probably from Pennsylvania, taking their mare, a handful of hogs, and a headful of dreams—going west. I saw them on one side of this nothing creek unloading the wagon, crossing, loading it all up again, and wondering if this was the last fording before nightfall.

The prairie is forever buffalo and Indian country to me. I don't see the stubborn little farm houses, I ignore the two-story combines and the giant grain bins and lean into the wind and the thick-stem grass—my hunting blood at pioneer level...my imagination searching for Sioux braves as I crest the rise in the prairie.

What I did see as I topped the rise was a handful of wild-eyed Labs flushing two dozen birds about three gunshots away; a sight only too familiar to the long-time Lab owner. But it's a glorious sight anyway, and one you won't often see unless you're a prairie pheasant hunter.

Iowa has a lot of famous crops, and although I can't speak for most of them, I can say that the pheasants are hard work. Iowa, as you may or may not know, has no downhill, and somehow the wind is always in your face, snatching away what little breath you have left from climbing and wading through what they call "grass."

I stop to rest a minute and watch some other hunters straggling across the fields of another farm. Now and then, far, far in front a bird flushes for no reason I can imagine—except that this is wild bird country, there's a restlessness in the November air, a need to move, and it touches me as well.

I trudge on a little more slowly and see that the dogs have slowed down as well. No need to hurry, there will almost certainly be birds as we come to the end of the field; it shouldn't be a surprise but somehow it always is.

I hear a close shot and see that my partner has tumbled a rooster. I quit looking for arrowheads and pay more attention to the quartering dogs. I'm ready to practice my early morning shooting lesson.

I'd missed a rather easy bird and felt I had to discuss it; why, I don't know since no one really cares or listens, but somehow in this nonsense I asked my farmer partner what chokes he likes for pheasants and he told me full and full. I said I thought modified would be enough and he told me why he disagreed.

"Watch," he said, "when the nest bird gets up it'll go like a rocket—but only for eight or ten seconds. He stops flying then and just glides, maybe adds a wingbeat or two if he needs it but that's all. Now you wait—don't shoot—until he stops flying and levels off and he's a lot easier even if he's a little farther out. Full and full will fetch him."

I did just that but it wasn't easy—watching a bird climb out like a fury and doing nothing for a few seconds. But I waited, took time to get my feet, get my cheek firmly planted on the stock and the butt where it ought to be on my shoulder. I leisurely—in comparison to my usual haste—swung through and had the great satisfaction of a clean headshot.

As they say, "Easy when you know how." I thought of all the pheasant hunting I'd done and no one had ever pointed out that eight to ten seconds of flight. Of course, it would have never occurred to me either, but it's as good a shooting tip as I've ever had; one of the few that make sense and really work.

Later that day I saw my "coach" miss a bird—both barrels. I smiled and said, "Those who can't do, teach."

He blushed and said, in his nice humble, almost shy, way, "That's about the first bird I've missed in two years."

"Maybe you were imitating me," I said, "just to make me feel better."

"No," he said, "I just honestly left the safety on."

I said that maybe that's why I'd missed a couple of birds earlier; he smiled right back and said, "Maybe…"

We went back to the farm for lunch and I wandered around poking my nose into the equipment sheds, dwarfed by tractors the size of small locomotives. I remembered my grandfather behind his team of dappled grays, the reins thrown across his broad shoulders so he had both hands free to steer the heavy plow. I remembered the neighbors helping with the hay, turning the rows with long-handled wooden rakes and laughing about who knew how to build a good haycock and who didn't. Different country and different times, but the worries and the hours have stayed about the same.

We ate our sandwiches and talked dogs and guns and birds. Most of us liked heavy loads and big shot sizes; 5s were the favorite, with a vote or two for 4s, and the pointing dog men liking 6s. Typical small talk, the arguments were always the same and we all enjoyed every minute of it; the small talk of friends, the stuff that bridged who else you might have been, and yet we were all the same—bird hunters.

I had two birds left for a limit and felt high and mighty about my eight-to-ten-second lesson. I was wondering what it would be like to never miss another pheasant—how I'd handle greatness—when I stepped on a rooster. By the time I had fired the second barrel he quit flying and started to glide. I heard a familiar voice call out, "That was a mighty short ten seconds!" Being smart for once I said nothing. Wait until the next bird, I thought to myself and wondered why in the name of Kimble and Bogardus I couldn't retain anything for a couple of hours. One of the Labs looked birdy and I watched him, saying ten seconds to myself. And it worked perfectly. I swore I'd never let another cock bird boss me around or frighten me into forgetting.

I was all done and had discovered both downhill and downwind. I headed for the truck, gleaning the ground for arrowheads again, with no success. Maybe the Sioux picked them all up, like saving the empties; maybe they weren't as careless as I am, maybe they were just great shots.

I liked walking through the standing corn, I liked the rustling sound and the way it arched over my head, almost protectively, and I understood why the pheasant felt safe from the hawks—so did I.

Almost at the end of a row I saw a big rooster running toward the open field and, the instant he was there, throw himself into the graying sky and cackle good-bye to me. I watched and counted to ten when he began to glide. He turned and settled into a willow thicket, safe at home with the doors shut and locked and he crowed one more time to say so.

There was less than an eyebrow of sun left; a handful of minutes until dark. From not too far off I heard a coyote, a rolling bark borne to me by the wind. Then I heard another, an answer surely. The small boy who loved the "penny dreadful" books about cowboys and Indians remembered that once the

Sioux called like coyotes on these prairies. I smiled to myself for questioning what was real, knowing that it's always real when the coyote calls in the dark…something is always listening fearfully in the dreadful silence that follows.

MICHAEL MCINTOSH

Michael McIntosh is one of the world's best-known writers on shotguns and shooting. He is shotgunning columnist for Sporting Classics, Shooting Sportsman, and Gun Dog, and a regular contributor to The Double Gun Journal and Wildlife Art News as well. In addition to best-selling gun books—Best Guns, The Big-Bore Rifle, A. H. Fox, and his latest, Shotguns and Shooting—he has also written books on sporting artists Robert Abbett, David Maass, and Herb Booth.

His lifelong fascination with pheasants has taken him from his boyhood cornfields of Iowa to the western prairies, from game farms in the East to Victorian shooting estates in England and hunting clubs in eastern Europe.

six

PHEASANT GUNS AND GUNNING

by Michael McIntosh

I shot my first pheasant in a cornfield north of Cedar Rapids, Iowa, with a Model 31 Remington pumpgun that belonged to my father. I was dressed in blue jeans, a wool shirt, laced leather boots, and a canvas hunting coat.

I shot my most recent pheasant on the Tisza Plain of Hungary, with a London sidelock gun, wearing breeks, Wellington boots, a starched tattersall-check shirt, necktie, and waxed cotton jacket. A loader stood behind me, ready with fresh cartridges so I didn't have to take my eyes off the birds streaming overhead.

It's hard to imagine more dissimilar circumstances centered on the same bird, but if I've learned anything from the many thousands of them I've shot in the nearly forty years since the first one, it's that the pheasant offers more diversity in gunning than any other game bird. And no other has influenced the modern game gun to a greater extent.

While it's not strictly true that game guns were invented for pheasant shooting, it is true that the best-quality London sidelock reached the peak of its perfection at a time when pheasant shooting was the most widely practiced form of gunning in England, so the pheasant certainly helped shape the ultimate nature of the gun.

In the late-Victorian and Edwardian eras, pheasants were the sport of royals and nobility; entire country estates were laid out and managed to provide demanding, high-quality shooting, and legions of gamekeepers were employed to ensure huge numbers of birds. While the native red grouse of northern England and Scotland exist only as wild populations on the bell-heather moors, pheasants are highly amenable to rearing and release. What began in the 1860s as a catch-as-catch-can affair of walking up local birds in whatever numbers nature provided was by the late 1880s a formalized sport involving beaters, stops, loaders, pickers-up, and others, supported by a vast system of intensive management. By 1900, twelve thousand birds were reared each year in the pheasantries of the royal estate at Sandringham alone, and countless thousands more at shooting estates all over the country.

What drove it all was the cachet conferred by the Prince of Wales, the social arbiter of the age. Because the man who would be King Edward VII loved shooting almost as much as he disliked riding and walking, pheasant shooting soon evolved from mere sport to an elaborate social institution of extravagant weekend shooting parties complete with five-course meals and costume balls. This environment created an unprecedented demand for fine guns, and under the patronage of virtually the entire upper level of British society, the London gun trade flourished as never before or since.

Although the hammerless sidelock gun was already nearing the endpoint of its evolution, pheasant shooting provided the impetus for its ultimate perfection. Driven birds offer a great deal of shooting over a relatively short time, so the ideal gun should be light enough that its weight isn't burdensome. But the best driven pheasants fly high and fast, so the gun must also be balanced for a smooth swing and steady control. For the same reason, it should also be closely tailored to the man who shoots it. The volume of shooting requires that it be both highly durable and mechanically efficient; the superb craftsmanship of the London gun trade ensured the one, and creativity enhanced the other in the form of ejectors and self- and assisted-opening actions. The volume of shooting also created practical reasons for building guns as identical pairs and sets. Finally, the customers' level of taste required the highest quality in aesthetics, fit, finish, and decoration.

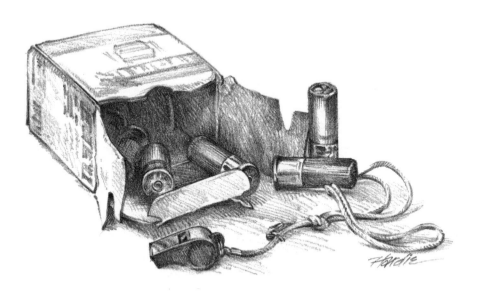

In short, the English gentry wanted only the best, and the English gun trade responded with the finest game guns ever built. Without the pheasant it might have happened anyhow, but probably not to the same extent nor in exactly the same way.

Given all this, logic would suggest that an English game gun is the ideal piece for pheasants. In some ways it is—or at least some of its characteristics are ideal for pheasants. But the diversity I mentioned earlier extends to the gun as well.

Driven shooting is wonderful sport, readily available and in many cases surprisingly affordable. But it doesn't exist in the United States. Some gun clubs occasionally stage what are generally called "Continental shoots," in which pheasants are launched from a tower or a hilltop and encouraged to fly over gunners waiting below; they can be fun, but these events bear little resemblance to classic English or European shooting.

What we have are umpteen zillion acres of farmland virtually crawling with wild pheasants, supplemented with dozens of game farms, hunting clubs, preserves, and other such places where pen-reared and liberated birds offer a quality of sport that ranges from so-so to first-rate. But in any case, whether the birds are hatched in a timothy hayfield or an incubator, classic American pheasant hunting is an entirely different game, and some of the differences reflect upon the optimal choice of gun.

As with all game birds, the keys lie in the nature of the animal itself and the ways it interacts with its environment. *Phasianus colchicus* is neither a wilderness bird nor a woodland dweller, although brushy woods edges can be favorite escape cover. Grass, grainfields, weedpatches, ditches, sloughs, and other such places dense at ground level are prime habitat, and in these places pheasants prefer to avoid danger by skulking around as quietly as cats. This is especially true of cocks. Hens generally are fond of hiding, burrowing into thick vegetation, and sitting tight. Cock birds, on the other hand, are great movers, astonishingly adept at playing cat and mouse or, if you push them out of the heavy stuff, able to take off like a herd of pronghorns.

Pheasant legs are long, heavily muscled, and reinforced at the thighs by thin, splinterlike sesamoid bones. These offer additional support for the ligaments and also enhance the angle of muscles to leg bones, giving the bird remarkably powerful leverage. With a stride of about eighteen inches, he's more than a match for any man who's not a trained sprinter, and he'll give even the fittest dog a good run for its money.

Their penchant for staying on the ground as long as possible is what makes pheasants so responsive to being driven. If the beaters are skillful—that is, if they stay fairly close together, move slowly, and don't make a great deal of noise—most of the birds in any given covert simply drift ahead of the line, bunching together until they come up against some barrier.

The most effective barrier, and the most common, is simply open ground; an innate fear of airborne predators makes pheasants reluctant to run out from under the protective canopy of tall grass, trees, or understory brush, and if they're prevented from turning back they have no choice but to fly.

This all works about the same way regardless of whether the birds are being pushed by a line of beaters with walking sticks or by a line of hunters carrying guns. We don't think of it as driven shooting—and in the European sense it isn't—but the approach involving battalions of hunters sweeping through cover toward blockers stationed at the end plays on precisely the same characteristics of the bird. In Iowa and the Dakotas and other wide-open places, the trick is to work toward some barrier, be it a field edge, a road, a fenceline, stream bank, or whatever, and pin the birds between two circumstances that make staying on the ground less than attractive.

A lone hunter, or a group of two or three, can use the same approach on a smaller scale, especially with the assistance of either a short-ranging flushing dog or a canny old pointer who knows the game of circle-and-pin. It's all a matter of exploiting the pheasant's habit of running away from a walking man.

They also fly away from a walking man or a flushing dog; therein lies an important difference between a pheasant that's truly driven and one that's booted up by the hunter himself, and here's where the nature of the sport influences the gun.

Actually, any gun can be effective on pheasants provided it is light enough to carry and handle comfortably, heavy enough to swing smoothly, balanced so that the muzzle doesn't jump and twitch, capable of a quick, controlled second shot, and efficient at patterning a reasonable charge of medium-sized shot. It certainly ought to fit the shooter, and the trigger should be crisp and light. Otherwise, it can be anything from a London best to the plainest Jane in gundom.

Thinking back, it occurs to me that I've shot pheasants with just about everything that shoots—side-by-sides, over-unders, pumps, autoloaders, and single-shots, even, in one instance, a bolt-action shotgun that an especially kind Iowa farmer loaned me when a couple of friends and I turned a college road-trip into an impromptu pheasant hunt. It handled with all the grace of a garden rake, but while neither it nor the penny loafers I was wearing would have been my first choices for gear, they both did the job.

I have also shot pheasants with guns of every bore size from 10 to .410, but even though the ones I hit properly fell equally dead, I have to say that walk-up pheasant hunting is really not a small-bore sport. Even in the hands of a truly expert shot, a .410 is a poor joke as a game gun; much as I love the 28-gauge, and as many pheasants as I've shot with it, it's a pheasant gun only for those with enough restraint to pick their shots with almost surgical care. For released birds on a game farm, it's a dandy; for wild pheasants in most of the real world, it's a gun to leave at home.

For workaday hunting, pounding the switchgrass and flogging the corn stubble, a 20-bore is as small as I care to go. Most 20s will handle an ounce of shot well enough to put a killing pattern on a pheasant-sized bird. A 16 will do it better yet and a

12 best of all. The typical 10-gauge is a bit much, but a chap I used to hunt with years ago had a lovely old Parker 10-bore that made a wonderful pheasant gun. It really wasn't any heavier than most 12-gauge repeaters, and with handloads of an ounce and one-quarter of No. 6 shot it was deadly as lightning and comfortable to shoot besides.

The most important part of a pheasant hunter's armament isn't the gun but rather the cartridges. Pheasants aren't nearly as hard to kill cleanly as ducks, but apart from turkeys they're tougher than any other bird you'll find in the uplands. A big cock bird can take an incredible pounding and still fly off to die somewhere far away. Break a wing and he'll run clear out of the country. Your best chance of putting him down and keeping him where he falls comes from hitting him with several pellets carrying enough energy to deliver a substantial blow.

Perhaps the greatest difference between driven and walk-up birds is that a driven pheasant is always flying toward the gun, either coming straight on or quartering. It's usually permissible to turn and shoot after they've passed overhead, but at least for the first shot, they're oncoming targets.

They will also be high birds; with beaters in front and other guns spread out on either side, safety demands that you pass up any bird lower than about forty-five degrees to the vertical. It's a rule strictly enforced, and the consequences of violating it can be serious. On a European shoot, I once saw an inexperienced gun swing on a low bird as it passed through the line of guns and bag two Italians and a guy from Florida with a single shot. By some miracle no one was badly hurt, but the aftermath was fraught with blood, hard feelings, a police investigation, and, as it happened on the very first drive, the loss of an entire day's shooting for everyone.

My point here, however, is that a high pheasant is a vulnerable bird. Oncoming, all its vitals are exposed—head, wings, breast, and belly. A high crosser is almost as vulnerable, and a high bird going away is showing you wings and belly. Driven birds can be remarkably hard to hit when they're flying high and fast, but if you can get the range it's fairly easy to deliver a killing shot, and unless they're unusually high—say, fifty yards or better—a 20-bore gun is perfectly adequate.

In walk-up hunting we don't see many high birds and even fewer incomers, and that changes the game considerably. We get mostly low crossing and going-away shots. Cock pheasants make such a great racket when they take off that it's easy to get rattled, poke the gun without mounting it properly, and shoot over the bird—or fail to accommodate a rising flight and shoot under—or get distracted by those long, streaming tailfeathers and miss behind. A shot missed marginally high or low may break a leg or a wing-knuckle, and one almost too far behind might put a pellet or two in the body, but all three are likely to result in lost cripples.

A pheasant flying straight away is virtually armor-plated. Its head is protected by the body, breaking a wing or leg is chancy, and the vitals are shielded by a wide, remarkably tough backbone. Unfortunately, going-away shots are the most common in walk-up hunting, and I've seen enough feathers to stuff a mattress raked off straightaway birds that kept right on going.

All this makes certain demands upon gun and cartridge. Besides being one you can shoot well, your gun needs to deliver a wide, even pattern at the ranges where you take your shots. Early in the season when cover is lush and a lot of callow, young-of-the-year birds are still in the field, improved-cylinder is as tight as you'll need; I like skeet or cylinder bore even better. Later on, when cover thins out and the survivors have grown wise and spooky, you'll find good use for a modified barrel. But beware the temptations of full choke; it's really useful only at ranges well past forty yards, and most upland gunners, myself included, can't shoot consistently worth a damn at those distances. Poking long shots at pheasants may bring down the odd bird now and then, but every one will be offset by a half-dozen lost cripples that you didn't even know were hit.

But as I said, the cartridges are even more important. For one thing, soft shot just doesn't get it, and neither does very small shot. Soft pellets are too easily deformed, either by being crushed when the powder charge ignites or by scraping the barrel as they go down the bore; deformed pellets quickly shed velocity and energy, fly erratically, and are therefore all but useless. So-called "promotional" cartridges are okay for targets and short-range, soft-bodied birds, but if pheasants are important to you, the extra dollar or two you'll have to pay for a box of top-quality shells is an investment in respect for the game. Personally, I'm willing to scrimp on target loads because target shooting is purely for fun—but never, ever on cartridges I intend to fire at birds. Hard shot is more expensive, but lost, crippled birds exact an even greater price from my soul.

Small shot is effective enough for driven pheasants at moderate distances. Put me in the right place and I won't hesitate to shoot them with woodcock loads. For field shooting, though, I want pellets with enough weight to carry plenty of energy out to the birds. That means No. 7½ at the least, and No. 6 is considerably better. To stand the best chance of bagging a pheasant you or your dog has flushed, you need to hammer him and hammer him hard. That means multiple hits with pellets of substantial weight.

But here's also where you have to get really hard-nosed and skeptical and dismiss all the blather you hear about "magnum" loads, whether it comes from ammunition makers' marketing departments or writers who don't know dog crap from Shinola about shotgun ballistics. The only way to effectively impart more energy to the bird you're trying to kill is to hit it with more pellets or heavier ones. Merely making light pellets fly faster doesn't work.

As a look at any ballistics table will show, the faster you start a round object moving through the atmosphere, the faster it slows down. Compare, for example, two pellets of the same size and weight—in this case No. 7½—leaving the muzzle at substantially different velocities.

Velocity (fps):		
muzzle	20 yards	40 yards
1,330	930	715
1,200	865	675

The 130-feet-per-second difference at the muzzle is reduced by half in the first twenty yards and amounts to only forty feet per second at forty yards. Velocity itself, however, never killed anything; what's important is energy. Notice how the same two pellets compare:

Energy (ft/lbs):		
muzzle	20 yards	40 yards
4.91	2.40	1.42
4.00	2.08	1.26

Here again, more than half the difference is erased in twenty yards and it's utterly negligible at forty yards. Believe me, .16 foot-pound of energy more or less won't affect a pheasant in the least. The only one who'll notice any effect from higher velocity is the shooter, because increasing velocity also increases recoil.

The point—which the magnum-heads don't seem to get—is to hit the bird harder, not the shooter, and the way to do that is to use heavier shot. This time, let's compare energies of a No. 7½ pellet, a No. 6, and a No. 5, all leaving the muzzle at 1,200 feet per second:

	Energy (ft/lbs):		
	muzzle	20 yards	40 yards
No. 7½	4.00	2.08	1.26
No. 6	6.20	3.49	2.23
No. 5	8.22	4.78	3.13

Clearly No. 6s carry a bigger punch than No. 7½'s at all distances and No. 5s even more yet. When I lived in Iowa and hunted pheasants often, I often shot No. 5s at late-season birds. They certainly are effective, but I'd advise against using them in anything smaller than a 12-bore gun. In the first place, a one-ounce charge of No. 5s contains roughly 170 pellets, which is getting close to minimal for good pattern density even in a 12-gauge, and the relatively long shot string from a 20 would make it awfully patchy. Besides, quite a few small-gauge barrels don't pattern pellets of No. 5 or larger very well.

And lest you be tempted—hoodwinked is a better word—by the fabled three-inch 20 and its 1¼-ounce shot charge, purported to deliver 12-gauge performance in a smallbore gun, let me tell you that it's possibly the worst cartridge ever conceived, for pheasants or any other bird. The ballistics are awful at any but point-blank range, where a skeet load is all you need, and in a lightweight gun the recoil is savage. If you want 12-gauge performance—and for all-around pheasant hunting I believe you need it—then use a 12-gauge gun. I say this having shot a few dozen pheasants with three-inch 20s—and having filed the experience away under the heading of "Long Ago and Never Again."

Stuffing more shot into a cartridge than the bore size can optimally handle is never a good idea, but this isn't to say that a fairly heavy charge can't be effective. In fact, my all-time favorite pheasant load is an ounce and one-quarter of No. 6s in a 12-gauge shell, backed by a 3¼-dram-equivalent powder charge for a muzzle velocity of 1,220 feet per second. It's the classic live-pigeon load (except that No. 7½ shot is standard for pigeons), and I've yet to find a 12-bore gun that won't pattern it beautifully. The recoil isn't bad, although I wouldn't want to use them on a driven shoot where the daily bag is three or four hundred birds; but for collecting a limit of two or three or four cocks, it's just dandy. The shot string is fairly short, the swarm very dense, and any pheasant that collects eight or ten No. 6s in the body is a dead one. If you can't find any $3\frac{1}{4}$-$1\frac{1}{4}$ cartridges made with 6s, try pigeon loads; they're almost as good. The denser pattern helps offset the smaller shot's lesser energy.

If you're a handloader, look up a good $1\frac{1}{4}$-ounce 12-gauge recipe that generates from 1,200- to 1,220-feet-per-second velocity. And pay special attention to the shot you use, because common bulk shot isn't hard enough for optimum performance on pheasants; what you want is lead alloyed with a 4 to 7 percent quotient of antimony. It will cost more, but it is money well spent. If you're not sure what's what, look for the word magnum on the bag; that's how most makers identify the hard stuff. You can use copper- or nickel-plated pellets if you want, but don't assume that plating alone makes soft shot any harder, because it doesn't. Only antimony does that. I have a notion that plated hard pellets may hold their shape a wee bit better by resisting abrasion as they rub against each other, but in purely practical terms I'm not sure it's truly worth the extra expense.

What I do know is that pheasants prompt me to give more thought to the guns and cartridges I use than do any other birds. Part of it is admiration for their sheer toughness, which is both physical and spiritual. As I've said, no other upland bird is more difficult to put down for the count, and even when you think you have, he can spring some surprises. I've seen more than a few pheasants fall limp as rags, to all appearances dead before they hit the ground, only to crawl off and hide so well that the dogs were hard-put to find them. I still have some faint scars left by a big Iowa cock bird I picked up by the neck years ago; I thought he was dead, but he still had enough juice to rake my left forearm with both feet.

Another came alive in my game pouch one time, literally forced his way out and tried to fly off. As I was wearing the vest at the time, it scared the bejesus out of me. We've all heard stories about stunned deer regaining consciousness inside automobiles; it's never happened to me, but I don't imagine the havoc is much more intense than having a live pheasant flailing around in your clothing.

There's more to it than just that extraordinary tenacity for life. A cock pheasant is the only bird I know that swears at you when you make him fly. You have to respect such a go-to-hell attitude, just as a look from those cold, bright, sulphur-yellow eyes is enough to let you know that you're dealing with a spirit that lies close to the nature of wildness itself. I've never tried to outwit a sly old white-tailed buck or stag elk on its own ground and never will, but I've played the game time and again with equally canny rooster pheasants who know their turf in better detail than I know my own house, and it never ceases to be a satisfying challenge, no matter which way it ultimately goes.

More than any other game bird, pheasants have represented milestones and markers in my life. For a long time I considered my birthday, December 7, to be the dividing line between two distinct forms of pheasant hunting, or at least it was in Iowa. From opening day till then it was fair-weather sport in nearly every sense—larking about the fields with a 20-bore gun after young, dumb birds that held tight and flushed close and generally behaved as if everything that happened was a great surprise.

Afterwards, though, the whole complexion was different, usually snowy, always cold, the annual cover beaten down, and the simpletons either gone to Sunday dinners or a damn sight smarter than they were just a few weeks before. Then was the time for a 12-gauge and a lot of shoe leather worn down plodding from one scrap of hard cover to the next, a time when brush pants lived up to their name and when a three-bird limit at the end of a long day was something special.

I haven't done that sort of thing very much lately. The nearest pheasant country is better than a half-day's drive from where I live now, and traveling on magazine assignments seems to leave less and less time each fall for that kind of prospecting anyway. But pheasants are still part of the picture, because for the past several years I've spent the first week of December shooting driven birds in Hungary. It's a more genteel pastime than plowing brush and decidedly easier on my increasingly cranky knees, but it exacts its own demands and confers its own special thrills.

As it happened, December 7, 1993, was the last shooting day of the trip, and I walked out through a cool, gray, foggy morning toward the first drive feeling a little weird in realizing that having forty-eight years on my head almost certainly meant that the midpoint of my life was well past. It didn't come as an especially gloomy thought, but it somehow reminded me to be more aware of the smell of the air and the crinkly sound of footfalls in the grass. By the time the drive began I was half-smiling to myself.

And then the first birds broke out of the trees far ahead, three or four veering toward the other guns ranged in a line to my left and a close-flying pair boring straight toward me, wings hammering for maximum altitude. Giving myself a silent word of admonition to try and do this right, I let them come into range, took a little step toward the invisible spot I had picked out, swung the barrels through the first one from tailfeathers to beak, touched the trigger, kept the muzzles going in the same butt-belly-beak-and-bang sequence on the second, and was pleased to no end to see two plump bodies arcing down and to hear moments later two muffled thumps just a couple of seconds apart.

My loader, a fine gentleman and sportsman named Tibor Tihanyi, whacked me on the shoulder and shouted something in Magyar that included the word bravo! and I felt every bit as good as I had in that Iowa cornfield thirty-five years before when I saw the look of pride and congratulation in my father's eyes.

A life doesn't have to be wealthy in order to be rich, nor even very long to be meaningful. All it needs is some pheasants in it.

TOM HUGGLER

Tom Huggler has written numerous books on the great outdoors, including a few on upland bird hunting, the latest of which is entitled A Fall of Woodcock *and is due out next summer. A long-time pheasant hunter, Huggler has chased ringnecks in Iowa, Montana, North Dakota, South Dakota, Nebraska, Kansas, Missouri, Ohio, and in his native Michigan, where, as he tells in the following story, his fascination with pheasants first got off the ground.*

Huggler is a past president and board chairman of the Outdoor Writers Association of America, current contributing editor to Outdoor Life, *and a regular contributor to* Gun Dog, Wing & Shot, Shooting Sportsman, *and many other magazines. You can catch him in action in his videos, "Pheasant Hunting with Tom Huggler," and "Grouse Hunting with tom Huggler," both available through Countrysport.*

seven

FORTY YEARS OF PHEASANT HUNTING

by Tom Huggler

ctober 1955: I wonder why the limit is only two rooster pheasants. There are so many birds and some of my uncles and older cousins have pumpguns that hold five big red shells with shiny brass bottoms, and they are good shots and always seem to get their limits within a few minutes after ten o'clock, which is when the pheasant season opens each October in Michigan. This year they let me out of school to eat the big breakfast with them at Uncle Andy's and Aunt Marge's, and then I got to ride up on dusty gravel roads from Flint to Reese in a place they call the Thumb. Jouncing along in the back seat of Uncle Andy's green 1949 Chevrolet sedan with the Irish setter that won't sit still and the road stirring my feet through thin-soled tennis shoes, I smell the Hoppe's No. 9 Solvent and the new leather boots and imagine my hand as a mitten to find the Thumb and to guess at how long the ride will take from the first knuckle to the second. At ten years I have lots of questions like that but am old enough to know to keep most of them to myself.

Cousin Art is the best shot of all and everyone knows it and maybe it is because of the small tin can they call a Poly-Choke on the business end of his J. C. Higgins 12-gauge. But Art says no. It's because he watches the leafy sugar beets for movement and keeps his eye on the stub tail of the cocker spaniel and is the first one to come up shooting and keeps shooting until the gun is empty. They say Art fired three shots one time at a rooster that flew into the open window of a barn, then killed the bird when it flew out the other side. But that was before my time. Today, I take my place in the line of hunters between my father and older brother. Soon, the guns going off sound like the battle scenes I watch on *The Big Picture* show on black-and-white television.

Art lets me hold the gas-operated semi-automatic (whatever that is) before he slams new shells into it. I can taste the tang of gunpowder and the barrel is hot and the gun is much heavier than the Red Ryder air rifle Dad gave me for Christmas last year and which I carry proudly, taking care—as I have been told repeatedly—not to point it at anyone. My father, who found this place near Reese after the War and who organized these annual opening-day family hunts, shoots a ringneck and lets me carry it. But the bird is not dead, and when I tell him as much he tells me to finish the job. After all, why do I think I'm carrying the BB gun?

The bird's golden eye is wide open and the bird is either very fierce or very frightened, warring emotions that I feel myself but don't understand (and perhaps never will understand) and so I cock the air rifle and pull the trigger and the pheasant kicks and then is still. Strong hands on my back and a mild Dutch rub on my crew-cut head commend the deed and welcome me into the fraternity of pheasant hunters.

My father's rooster is now my rooster. It is a bird as beautiful in death as it was in life: the painted head with its blood-red cheek patches, sleek crown of emerald, white throat ring. The black-tipped bronze breast feathers changing like an oil slick

from purple to green to blue. The pointed tailfeathers with twenty-seven bar markings on one and twenty-six on another. The golf-tee spurs that prick my fingers.

Forty years later I will admire pheasants with the same wonder and question how anyone can call them "ditch parrots" and really mean it. I will never stare again into the eye of a doomed cock bird without seeing myself, and that is why I pick my shots carefully and why I hold the birds away when it becomes necessary to dispatch them. I have learned to do this by suffocation, crushing the rib cage between thumb and middle finger, inserting them under the wing-to-body sockets. Such unfortunate business is over quickly that way, and it is infinitely better than the barbaric whack against the gun barrel, more respectful than a twisting of the neck.

So now I am a hunter of birds bigger than sparrows and my coming of age occurs during the last great wave of pheasants in Michigan—the mid-1950s when hunters killed more than a million ringnecks each year. And although I won't get my first gun—the Mossberg 20-gauge, three-shot bolt action with the red-and-green safety tab—until junior high school, I can still go pheasant hunting. On autumn afternoons when the lumbering school bus deposits me at my rural home, I run up the driveway, change into jeans, slip on extra woolen socks to fill the too-big boots, grab the air rifle from the gun cabinet next to my father's L. C. Smith double, let out Queenie the English setter, and race across the back yard to the enormous weed fields beyond.

There I chase Queenie who chases the pheasants that erupt in waves, and sometimes I am a long way from home when Mother calls to supper. Because my father gets home long after dark, he knows nothing about the imaginary limits I shoot each day, nor does he know I have undone Queenie's natural staunchness, and on the weekends when he gets angry and calls the dog a dumb-ass for busting birds, I am too ignorant to know it is my fault.

But those mystic experiences—the white dog rocking across the weed stubble, plumed tail flowing, pivoting suddenly on its nose, its ghostlike form slamming to perfect attention, the glorious confusion of wings and colors, all of which have nothing and yet everything to do with me—are reasons I love the setter breed today and why I won't tolerate loose dogs and looser points.

October 1962: She has agreed to go pheasant hunting with him, after church, if her father doesn't mind, and she doesn't think he will mind because, after all, he hunts pheasants too. Everybody does, don't they? But Daddy says there aren't as many birds as there used to be, and that's too bad because he finally has a good dog, a "Loo Ellen setter"—she hopes she's saying that right—named Captain. She's sure Daddy will take him hunting with Captain some day.

Fingers trembling, the young man hangs up the phone. The feeling—an odd constriction in the chest, a sensation of hollowness somewhere below the chest—is back. Years later, he will say "vulnerable" in deference to the self-help books, and he will associate the feeling with the loss of control, at once abhorrent and attractive, that you experience upon putting your future in the hands of another. He is a high school senior, she a sophomore, and they have been dating for two months. He will pick her up at one o'clock, in his father's Corvair, which he must return by five.

He brings Pepper, his father's new dog, a hard-running fool of a black Labrador with a steel trap for a mouth. His father had traded a Herter's shotshell reloader with a cracked shot tube for the dog, and who can say who got the better deal? The young man's 20-gauge Mossberg bolt-action has evolved into a 12-gauge 870 Wingmaster pump, a gun he bought from Uncle Andy for fifty dollars, or seventy-five hours of bagging groceries at the local supermarket.

Greeting him at the door is her father. He is a bear of a man but friendly and certainly likable except for that know-ing, discomfiting look that creeps into his passive blue eyes. The topics are far ranging: the disappointing pheasant crop, the Lions-Packers game (which is why he won't be hunting to-day), and the way Kennedy and Krushchev are giving each other the finger over Cuba.

After the obligatory delay, she appears, a blue turtleneck cheating the smooth, white hollows of her shoulders but reveal-ing the curve and swell of her breasts, prizes he has been allowed to touch but not see. He wonders how she squirmed into those jeans and wonders, too, if he will get a measured breath inside the confines of her family's living room with her father looking not at her but at him. Then, finally, they are in the little car backing out the driveway with the Lab's hot breath on his neck and its pink tongue panting.

In the field rank with weeds not far from home, he and the Lab are all business, and for once, the dog decides to obey. She follows a few steps behind and he feels her eyes upon his back and he straightens his shoulders. They find the first ring-neck in a cut cornfield next to a sea of pumpkins that lie, ripe and unpicked for Halloween, on the thinnest of vines, shocked and shriveled from the frost. The bird detonates off the dog's nose and barely escapes the powerful snapping jaws only to col-lapse in another explosion, this one a burst of feathers. Pepper returns the bird, a young cock, and gives it up after a minimum of threats from him. She is very happy for him and she wants to carry the pheasant now and the sinking feeling in his stomach is dangerously close to utter helplessness.

Later, he kills a second rooster and knows he should stop at the limit, but how do you brake emotions so powerful and so perfect even when you know they will make you feel bad inside later? The third ringneck is barely out of the grass when he hesitates a second, then shoots it. She cannot easily carry more than two birds, so he puts this one in his game bag and the warm weight that tugs at his shoulders is not unlike a touch from her hands.

The fourth ringneck comes much later when the sun is down and the sky is turning to rose. She sees the cock first, picking it out from the covey of drab hens in the failing light and hollers "Rooster" even as he is swinging through the flock. A jet of fire spits from the gun muzzle and the crippled bird hits the ground running and he knows he shouldn't have shot, should not have stretched even further beyond legal bounds. But the dog saves him from the worst sin of all, that of diminishment in her eyes, and back at the Corvair he opens the front-end trunk and lays out the cocks—one, two, three, four—in a row.

He knows how rare are the days when dog and man are so aligned in thought and action. He is happy, certain in the fact that he will never again kill four ring-necked pheasants with four shots. Clearly, this is a cup filled to the brim, but it can be filled beyond the brim. It is a day meant for taking, and he knows the way and she is willing. Her warm hands are soft, her fingers strong. They use his hunting coat. For weeks afterward he can faintly detect Here's My Heart perfume in the liner.

Later, as the stars come out and they don their cold jeans, they laugh at how the curious Lab, locked inside the Corvair, has steamed the windows. Much later, after he has taken her home—to her father's relief—and has dealt with his own father's anger at his being so irresponsibly tardy (with no thought whatever for his worried mother), he cleans the pheasants in his parents' basement. As he takes the slippery kernels of corn from the birds' crops and rolls them between his fingers he thinks of her and wonders if things will ever be that way, or ever the same way again.

It was the only time she hunted pheasants with him, although she said she appreciated the shotgun he bought her. After their children were born, she resented his going, especially the longer trips that took him beyond the Mississippi. But those trips became necessary when Michigan's pheasant harvest tumbled from half a million birds to two hundred thousand, then from two hundred thousand to half that (although some said the DNR was lying, that even less pheasants were being taken). Iowa, South Dakota, Kansas, and Nebraska—the Big Four farming and ranching states—still produced harvests of a million birds each and more, and when he no longer found himself wishing for calamities, natural and not so natural, to befall her, he was drawn to those places and to North Dakota and eastern Montana in the way that a surface-to-air missile seeks heat.

He learned that pheasant hunting had also changed. That what had once been easy limits of fat, arrogant row-crop birds that hunkered in the milo and cut corn until hunters and their dogs routed them had evolved into a free-range prairie ringneck—the prize of prizes for stealth and cunning. He discovered that birds knew he was coming when he closed the car door a half mile away. Even though ringnecks were more plentiful than at home, sometimes an all-day tramp produced few if any tailfeathers sticking from the game bag. Often, he witnessed defiant roosters, growing smaller in the distance, pointing their tails at him and cackling with laughter.

December 1984: A late-season foray to Iowa is typical of those traveling years. The 540 miles from southern Michigan to Williamsburg are tedious. More so when the land has been hard bitten by winter, and the early-season hunters have said that pheasants are down this year. Game biologists, ever mindful of public relations and the source of their paychecks, wince over this latter news. After all, the summer surveys they prepared said pheasant numbers would be stable or even somewhat improved over last year. That is what the biologists told the outdoor writers who in turn told the hunters, and so when the hunters come back short of limits, they curse the biologists, the writers, the chuckholes in the Illinois stretch of Interstate 80, and they forget to stop in the Amana colonies and buy something for the wife who was not happy with their leaving the day after Christmas.

The hum of asphalt and the click of expansion joints on the freeway make me glad to go. Over my shoulder I catch the setter bitch's eyes. Lady Macbeth pleads gratitude and anticipation at the same time. The other setter, Chaucer, a young male, is chewing on something, possibly the Morris shooting gloves I left too near the wire kennel. Holly, the yellow Lab, is sleeping. She always had more sense than the others.

Through the truck-plugged Chicago corridor a light rain is falling. One of every four cars carries Christmas presents, some still wrapped. The truck battery is weak and so I leave it running while I pump gas and get coffee. By western Illinois the storm is well behind, but the sky is a dirty pewter. Dull-green fields of winter wheat are punctuated by black, freshly plowed fields. I pass the huge sign for the massage parlor—a converted mobile home—at Peru and the round barn two miles east of Geneseo. Near Coal Valley a ragged string of seventeen Canada geese floats across the highway. A little farther on, a duck appears frozen in a pond. At East Moline, the sky plunges into blackness. At nine o'clock I check into the motel where Larry Brown has been waiting since dark.

Next morning over breakfast at the Landmark Restaurant ("Middle America" the sign says) Larry, a native Iowan, confirms that birds are down. He is averaging three hours of hunting for each rooster killed. Last year it was only two hours. Prepare for tough sledding, Larry warns.

It's okay. We've had good years too. Like 1979, when Gene and Larry and I shot twenty-six ringnecks. That was the year I flew into Madison, then drove down with Gene in his old Chevy with the bad muffler. Later, I wrapped our frozen birds with several days of the *Wisconsin State Journal* and somehow North Central Airlines got them back to Michigan, along with the borrowed shotguns and that ground-eating setter of mine that someone said should have been rerouted to Sacramento.

Today is poor weather. No wind. Heavy fog. It is thirty-five degrees and what snow is on the ground will soon melt. What sloughs we can see through the scrim of light look as though a giant has raked his fingers over the earth, leaving cottonwood and other trees to spring from the furrows. By legal shooting time we arrive at the farm of Robert and Shirley Montz, who cash-crop five hundred acres and raise hogs.

Year-end pheasants head for the toughest, nastiest cover around—those damnably delightful sloughs. Besides towering cottonwoods, the sloughs hold horseweed, giant ragweed, burdock, cocklebur, often cattails, sometimes phragmites. All morning we scrape mud gobs from our Bean boots. There are pheasant tracks along streaks of snow in the sloughs, but these are tough, hunter-hardened birds. The three of us move a dozen hens but neither hear nor see a rooster. Three years earlier we shot thirteen on this very farm.

At lunch Mrs. Montz confirms what we have long suspected: She is the finest cook in southeast Iowa. Roast beef, corn, potatoes and gravy, salad, peach pie, and ice cream await. Like threshers, we table up and fall to. In the afternoon we hunt the 160-acre farm of Barry and Denise Render, but there are no roosters on the Render place where the air is heavy with the odors of sour silage and pig manure. By day's end we are tired and spattered with mud. The dogs are played out, too. Jake, Larry's pointer, and Macbeth exchange growls but neither has the energy to fight. The tip of Jake's tail is bleeding from thrashing about in the sloughs all day. At the motel four men from Port Huron, Michigan, don't want to talk about the day's poor hunting.

In bed, my left thigh is twitching uncontrollably. Sometime close to dawn, the excruciating pain of a charley horse awakens me and I dress and go outside. A cold west wind and a starless sky threaten snow. Out on Interstate 80 the diesel long-haulers, headlights bobbing, are playing follow the leader. The dogs, spilling from their air freight kennels, stretch and pee and sniff each other.

At the Landmark truck stop we know the menu by heart: Smokey & the Bandit, Kiss My Grits, 16-Wheeler Pile-Up. I order Diesel Fuel Ya Up but can't eat all of the half-pound of chopped beef, two eggs, hash browns, and small mountain of toast. The dogs are thankful. At six-thirty we join the eastbound sweep of traffic on the interstate.

On the farm of Dean Wood, not far from the 800-inmate, maximum-security prison near Anamosa, I scratch down a cackling rooster that Macbeth magnificently pointed. The bird is not killed cleanly and flies on a hundred yards before dropping into a slough. Macbeth stickpins it again, but this time she's hidden in the tall grass and I run right past her. Larry moves in to see Jake backing my setter. I miss that scene plus the ensuing excitement when the rooster flushes as though untouched. Larry shoots that bird. Later, I redeem myself on a crossing rooster, left to right.

One of the pheasant hunter's joys, we agree, is finding out-of-the-way lunch stops such as Harker's Tavern in Amber. A pork tenderloin basket here is a whopping $2.10 and, much to our surprise, Old Milwaukee is served on tap. I catch Larry looking at his watch. He catches me clearing my throat. Harker's is a converted general store with ceiling fans that turn lazily and a wooden floor of one-by-four-inch planks. On the wall a curled bullwhip is flanked by old lumbering tools. Two video games are thankfully silent. The crack of struck pool balls would be a more fitting sound except that no one is playing pool either. Two poorly mounted deer with dust-covered eyes watch us and I wonder if we'll scrap the afternoon hunt and order beer after all.

After lunch we hunt on a farm outside Anamosa and get up two hens but no roosters. At the motel that evening Larry and I clean our morning birds next to an Indiana hunter who has been coming here for nine years. "Today was our worst day," he complains. "One bird for three guys."

Next morning at the Landmark, two older men at the adjacent counter are having a breakfast conversation.

"Well, another new year is just around the corner. Think it will end up better'n this one?"

"I dunno. I hate to sound like a pessimist but don't see how it'll be better."

"I started my business in '35. But it's harder today to get started. Takes more money, for one thing."

"Hah! You're lucky you had *any money* then at all."

"That's true, but we had to heat the store with corn cobs the first couple of years."

"Hah! You're lucky you had corn cobs to burn. We didn't have nothin'."

Today, we head out south and west to the sprawling Rathbun Public Hunting Area about a hundred miles away. The temperature is below freezing again and a breezy wind is coming from the northwest. County roads are littered with mud from tractors still working fields late in the year. Rows of disks from an enormous field cultivator gleam like a phalanx of warrior shields from some belligerent city-state in old Mycenae.

Larry shoots a cock bird that takes to wing so close it threatens to cut off his legs. I bounce a tight knot of bobwhite quail, but the dozen birds fly across a small but deep river to safety. The only other excitement occurs when I stick my light pickup in a grassy field. Two other hunters help Larry push me out, but I forget to retrieve the floormats I had slipped under the rear wheels for traction. Our tally for the day? One rooster. For the trip? Three.

Next morning we travel Interstate 80 east to Iowa City, passing the Peterbilts, the Macks, and the White Freightliners that creep and stretch along like various species of insects with small heads and bulging thoraxes. Safe and anonymous behind shining eyes of glass, the drivers are immobile, impassive. Yet ten miles south on Highway 218 enroute to Crawfordsville, we note that an oncoming farmer in a pickup will raise at least an index finger, if not a whole hand, to acknowledge that he does not occupy the planet alone.

Crawfordsville, population 288 people. "Birthplace of the Republican Party," according to the sign outside the village. Hawkeye State citizens take an acute interest in things decidedly Iowan. Headlines in this morning's *Des Moines Register:* "Iowa Man Killed in Michigan" (I'm glad it wasn't "Michigan Man Shot in Iowa"). In Iowa, with its dearth of major-league sports teams, 70 percent of the people follow college football and high school wrestling with the same intensity that Wednesday-night bingo fans invade the VFW hall. In Iowa they call their coaches "Hayden" and "Lute" and "George" as though they were next-door neighbors, and there are basketball hoops on barns and garages and driveway turn-arounds.

In the Olds-Swedeville area Robert Madden and his son, Ken, whom Larry knows from the Army Reserve, work three farms in a hog-raising enterprise. The ground froze again last night, but a waxy sun in a delft-blue sky promises to undo the earth once more. Bean boots just don't cut it over chisel-plowed clods of black dirt as slick as oiled anthracite. We flush a white-tailed doe at the first farm and a hen pheasant at the second. On the last stop of the hunt, we hit pay dirt. A big ringneck, its face as colorful as a clown's, bursts noisily from the cover and into the sun where we can't see to shoot. But we mark him down a quarter mile away and when he comes up again, this time on Larry's side of the stream, two other gaudy cock birds are suddenly in the air with him. Larry folds the tent on one, and I nail one of the others.

Later that afternoon, before I turned the truck east for the long run home, we compare notes. We have two birds apiece and have spent about two hundred dollars each, not exactly the kind of return on investment you announce out loud at home.

"Through some quirk in the law," Larry says, "the fifty-dollar license you bought is good for all of 1985. So you'll have to come back next fall."

And I will. No matter what the game biologists or outdoor writers say about pheasant-hunting prospects.

December 1994: Legal game in thirty-five states and six Canadian provinces, pheasants are hunted by some 4 million sportsmen and women who spend 35 million days afield every year. Still, we will never return to the Soil Bank days of forty years ago when 62 million acres were enrolled in America and when South Dakota alone boasted a standing crop of 15 million pheasants and when hunters killed 3.2 million of them.

Even so, it is in fields near home where I most enjoy hunting pheasants now because the experience reminds me of a time when life was simpler and easier although we missed going to war with Russia by an eyeblink and, who knows, I could have been in one of the first boats leaving Miami. I was certainly the right age. I lucked out with the Vietnam draft, too, only because I was a married father before President Johnson's August 1965 edict.

Anyway, the ringneck is holding its own in places like South Dakota and Iowa and coming back in places like Minnesota and Michigan, although the numbers of birds are relative. In South Dakota the current population stands at about 5 million. In Michigan the annual harvest has crept back to about two hundred thousand birds from a 1986 low of only eighty-four thousand. Mild winters and habitat improvement—thanks to 35 million acres enrolled in the national Conservation Reserve Program and the efforts of Pheasants Forever, an organization of seventy thousand hunter-conservationists in more than four hundred chapters across the pheasant belt—have ringnecks doing well enough for us Michigan hunters to enjoy a special, limited season in December.

Last December four friends and I spent a balmy morning chasing home-grown roosters in hopes of getting some footage for a pheasant-hunting video I was making. As we loaded guns in the farmer's front yard, one of my friends suddenly pointed to the immense field of winter wheat across the road. One hundred yards into the six-inch-high green wheatgrass was a small patch of weeds. A cock pheasant had stuck its showy head out from the weed protection. "Would you look at that?" another person in our group said. Then, as though on cue, the rooster dashed into the wheat field. Three other ringnecks sprinted after him in single file. Heads high, spear-like tails straight up, the panicked birds looked like running check marks. Streaking parallel to the road for fifty yards or so, they suddenly took to wing, sailed across the road, and landed in the middle of a forty-acre CRP field.

"Can you believe that?" someone said. "One for each of us."

"Wish I could have had the tape rolling," said Jim, the cameraman.

We unloaded my young setter, Sherlock, formed a cup shape twenty yards apart with Jim a few steps behind, and moved down into the heavy grass where the birds had vanished. The first cock rocketed out before my excited dog, nose afire with pheasant scent, could set a point. Ed stopped the bolting bird with a load of copper-plated 6s. Moments later Sherlock locked up in a classic pose—the kind of point that always reminds me of a quivering bow, tightly drawn. The cackling ringneck bolted for the sky, and Norris was in the best position to shoot, which he did, stopping the bird in mid-sentence.

I had traced both roosters without firing, and when the third cock boiled out, I was ready with my little over-under; the bird died before he hit the ground. Somehow, my rookie setter kept his cool in all this confusion, at least long enough to point a long-tailed ringneck for my neighbor, Fred, an older man who had not shot a pheasant in many years.

In fifteen minutes we had our one-bird limits, and still more pheasants—hens and cocks—came rousting from that forty-acre field and Jim, the cameraman, filmed us pointing empty shotguns at them, then borrowed a gun and made good on his own license. It was the kind of action that can take a long-time pheasant hunter back many years. Two weeks later, after the season had ended, the landowner's son called to tell me he saw five roosters and God only knows how many hens picking grit along the gravel road that runs by the farm.

I can be there in the amount of time it takes me to sip a cup of coffee brewed and poured in my own kitchen. So this fall—the 100-year anniversary of the introduction of Chinese pheasants to Michigan—I'm going back to that field and other fields near home. True, the slim 28-gauge I favor these days is heavier than a BB gun. But not much heavier.

CHRIS DORSEY

Chris Dorsey was born, raised, and educated in Wisconsin where he first developed his love-hate relationship with pheasants. He worked in Los Angeles as the senior editor of Petersen's Hunting *before becoming executive editor of* Ducks Unlimited. *His books include* Hunt Wisconsin, The Grouse Hunter's Almanac, Pheasant Days, Wildfowler's Season, *and* Game Days. *His freelance works have appeared in numerous national magazines including* Writer's Digest, Sports Afield, Field & Stream, Outdoor Life, Sporting Classics, *and a host of others. He's currently at work on another title on upland bird hunting to be released in 1996. Though he has hunted birds in ten countries, he's found none more difficult to subdue than a late-season rooster—something his setters could confirm.*

eight

FOOTPRINTS IN THE SNOW

by Chris Dorsey

Some places can be found by reading a map, others by following your heart. To get to pheasant country, look for the hints. The eager expression of a setter takes me back to a South Dakota prairie in the blink of an eye. A fragment of corn leaf stuck in a game vest reminds me of an Iowa farm as quickly as I can change thoughts. Add two inches of new snow to the city streets in which I live and I'm instantly transported through time to the Wisconsin marsh where I met my first ringneck one snowy December morning. The sounds of a dog bell or the taste of a cold wind often have the same effect.

To get the most out of pheasant country, you must learn to enjoy its many elements. Picking up a leftover ear of corn and shucking its kernels into a pile of gold has a rhythmic therapy like whittling a piece of willow. There is also comfort in imagining a pheasant making an easy meal of such toil. Then there is the satisfaction of napping against a fencepost following a long morning hunt, letting an equally tired bird dog pillow its head on your lap, or watching frost burst off goldenrod as a dog runs through cover with a windshield-wiper tail.

The sport is most memorable when a hunter finds himself in the company of a grand bird dog. Pheasant hunting with a dog is a partnership, a contract between man and beast written in genes. A pheasant dog is a creature of many talents. It knows how to pull cockleburs out of its pads and has a knack for writhing through even the thickest cover. Such a dog also learns to distinguish between pheasant cover and mere weeds. Don't be surprised if a seasoned pointer runs past a bird, hooks around it, and traps the runner between itself and the hunter. Such canine trickery is an imprecise game, so the dog may peer up at its master as if to say, "I could use some help with this one, boss." Some might offer that a pointer shouldn't be used to hunt pheasants, that these running birds will ruin the dog, but people also suggested that Babe Ruth was too rotund to play baseball.

A bonafide pheasant dog further knows how to tote a rooster. Through painful lessons, it learns to pick up a wounded bird by the back, keeping the switchblade spurs at bay. A seasoned dog squeezes the air from a flapping cock bird without disemboweling it during the retrieve. When it comes to range, the best pheasant dog ventures just far enough to find birds for the gun, but it must be understood that a rooster obeys no rules. A distinction most hunters miss is that it's the bird—not the dog— that normally dictates the pace of a hunt. While we may dream of close-flushing pheasants, it takes but a few encounters with hunters to change sitting birds into sprinters.

I was just a pup the first time I hunted behind a skilled pheasant pointer, an English setter by the name of Nasa. The Belton was owned by Gary Wilson, a middle school conservation teacher whose classroom looked like a wingshooter's den adorned with pheasant and grouse tails and pictures of hunts past. I was a neophyte who watched in wonder at the synergy between the two seasoned bird chasers. The duo possessed the meter and tempo of good verse. The poetry of the experience was wasted on my youth, however, as it was like expecting a ten-year-old to appreciate Keats.

It wasn't until I began to indulge in training my own bird dogs that I understood the degree of communication between

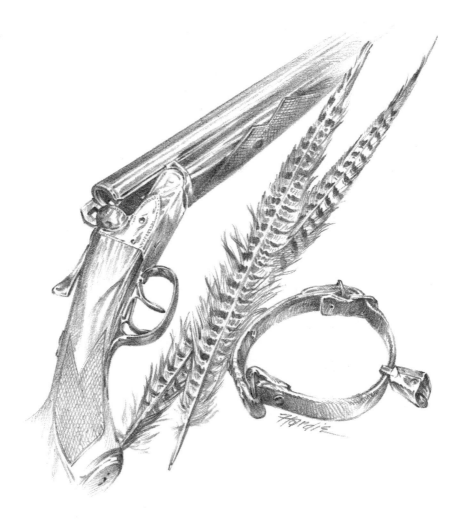

Gary and Nasa, and the amount of field time necessary to achieve such chemistry. With pheasant dogs, as with most things in life, it's a good idea to know something about the subject before you offer counsel to others. Until you have raised and trained a gun dog of your own, reserving comment on another dog's performance is the wisest course to self-preservation.

While any pheasant hunt is worthwhile, some are more memorable than others. Add snow to pheasant country and you may discover magic, for a pheasant in the powder becomes a new bird. Painted against the white of the winter palette, a rooster's plumage seems almost surreal. To track a pheasant in the snow is to see the ringneck as a bird dog might, step by step, cover by cover. How unnerving it must be for a bird, haunted by the malevolent shadow of the hunter, to discover that it can't outrun its tracks. When you follow a track to a small thicket of stems, walk around the vegetation. If no trail departs, it can only mean that the bird has abandoned the run and is hoping you'll pass by. There is electricity in such a moment; a hunter knows he has only to step into the cover to unearth the bird.

Indeed, fresh snow is an invitation from St. Hubert to track ringnecks. Each print is a clue in a game of hide-and-seek that is as old as the relationship between predator and prey. A new snow is nature's way of opening a door into the world of the ringneck.

It was the Thanksgiving after my twelfth birthday that I discovered just how memorable these days can be. Four inches of heavy packing snow painted our marsh in a thick coat of satin. The air was wet and cold. Steam rolled out of my setter's nostrils like plumes of dragon smoke.

I slipped the bell on Thor's collar more out of habit than practicality, for wet snow would soon collect in it, turning it into little more than a crude ornament dangling from his neck. Thor knew to stay at heel as we walked out of the yard, clearing the garden and the withered tomato vines climbing above the snow like the legs of so many dead spiders. We then traversed a football field of corn stubble that framed the marsh. The two of us knew every plant in the wetland, having logged enough hours there to qualify as residents of the biome.

The great marsh was severed by the Union Pacific Railroad. The east side was the largest and most productive stretch of pheasant cover. In the midst of this section was a bog with ankle-busting hummocks into which roosters liked to vanish. Traversing this expanse was treacherous, and I came to despise the birds that slipped into the bog to escape. There was also a ten-acre patch of tillable ground sitting like an island in the wetland. A local farmer planted the field when conditions were dry enough. In wet years—which outnumbered the dry springs— the cornstalks grew to about popcorn height and ultimately rendered nothing more than another government crop-damage check. The rest of the slough consisted of sedges, switchgrass, and cattails interspersed with the occasional copse of pussy willow. It was as if a pheasant had been consulted on the composition of the marsh—a perfect mixture of food and cover.

As we crossed the creek lining the west side of the wetland, Thor looked up at me, waiting for the tap on the head that was his signal to hunt birds. I walked a few more feet before releasing him, for even at my tender age I knew it was important that the dog get its cue to hunt from its master, not the other way around. He was soon bounding through the brush as he always did, as if late for an appointment. Looking down, I spied a solitary pheasant track weaving through the goldenrod. I wondered how close the bird might be, if it could hear or see me, and whether it knew it was being followed.

The new snow made the tracking easy, for there were no other trails to confuse the equation. My eyes scanned ahead to see how far I could spot the track, trying to anticipate where the bird might flush. I lost the prints for a moment, but spotted a twitch in the grass ahead. Thor had already located the bird and the tip of the setter tail whipped back and forth like that of a cat about to pounce. All that I could see was the clocklike tick in the switch, and it was all I had to see to know that Thor was waiting for me to circle ahead of him and stir the bird skyward. Thor's style wouldn't earn him accolades, but his flagging was a welcomed sight to me.

I popped the safety on and off, stretched my arms out and then back to make sure there was enough play in the stiff denim coat to mount the gun without snagging the butt in my armpit, and shuffled ahead of Thor, repeating the phrase "whoa buddy, whoa buddy." The words did more to soothe my nerves than they did to calm and steady the dog. The tail twitch ceased as Thor braced for the imminent flush with the tension of a goalie expecting a slapshot. I kicked the grass in a series of short steps until I reached the dog. Thor left his half-steady pose and frantically leaped ahead into the cover, plunging his nose under shocks of dead straw as if to say, "Trust me, there's a bird in here somewhere. I ain't lyin'." Just then, a rooster flushed ten yards behind me, having somehow avoided my upland shuffle. I spun and fired the first shot, killing only air space. The second load of 6s interrupted his whirring cadence.

It wasn't long before Thor had spit out the last of the pheasant feathers, and I wandered across another set of tracks. Each trail tells a story in the snow. The close footsteps and indiscriminate meandering of this track told me that the bird was in no hurry to get anywhere. At one point it stopped to peck a foxtail, dusting the snow below the stem with hundreds of the plant's pepperlike seeds. Another ten feet into the track, however, and the prints grew far apart, heading in a straight line toward a quagmire of cattails. This was the point at which the bird undoubtedly heard my earlier shooting. Even in the recesses of its atavistic memory it surmised that nothing good could come from such a sound.

Thor headed toward the next most promising patch of goldenrod and looked at me funny when I took a perpendicular course toward the cattails. This time I brought Thor to heel and focused on tracing the spoor with the concentration of a Masai tracker stalking a simba. The bird was hidden somewhere in the catacomb of cattails. The frosted stems resembled a cattail cake. Beneath the insulation was an intricate series of tunnels used by everything from muskrats and mink to fox and pheasants. But this bird chose to follow the more open deer trails traversing the cover, simplifying what could have been an impossible task of following it through the maze.

With each rustling step into the cover, I waited for the flush that I knew could come at any moment, but that I also knew would surprise me nonetheless. The commotion of a rising pheasant stuns the nerves like a sudden slap of ice water on a hot day. I was as ready for my flush of adrenaline as any mortal could be. Still, the tracks continued. I could see the bird vividly in my mind's eye, imagining it slinking along in that deceptive half crouch in which a rooster can outrun a bird dog. Before I Zenned-out, the ringneck broke through the canopy of snow like a submarine-launched warhead, vectoring toward the next section of land. The sound of flapping wings bursting through the cattails incited a flush response from another half-dozen birds. The unexpected ringnecks were so distracting that I managed merely to fire a distant shot at the last of the four departing roosters—an unsuccessful shot at that. I can think of no other time, however, when stalking has been so fraught with anticipation and my senses as a hunter so keen.

Entering pheasantdom today is an infinitely more complicated affair than it once was. In the case of upland gear, that isn't an altogether unwelcomed revelation. A well-known American writer once nearly ruptured a disk trying to extract himself from one of the early Japanese economy cars. Upon completing the task, he took a breath and said to the driver, "The person who designed this car must have had the human body *described* to them." This is much the sentiment of many pheasant hunters who, for far too long, endured the discomforts of poorly designed apparel. Too many early sporting clothing designers didn't know the difference between ergonomics and economics.

Brush pants made of canvas were the rage when I grew up. This was the best you could get, the crème de la crème. Problem was, the heavy canvas required to keep thorns off one's hide often absorbed melted frost, rain, and water from slogging through a marsh. If it was cold enough, this moisture would freeze, and walking in ice pants was infinitely more uncomfortable than hiking in, say, swamped waders. In recent years, designers have come to appreciate the fact that human legs bend at the knee, and that it's important to wear flexible britches when high-stepping through dense vegetation. Lighter, stronger, and improved waterproof materials have allowed hunters to remain more mobile, better protected, and drier in cover.

Jackets are another matter. A friend is convinced that elastic shell loops are the creation of ammunition manufacturers, because cartridges forever slip out of the loose holdings. Sewing elastic shell loops to a quality jacket or vest is akin to adding a wooden bumper to a Mercedes. I'll keep my shells in deep pockets or leather loops, thank you.

When it comes to pheasant guns, the best are those that feel as though they're carrying themselves over the course of a long day's hunt. Such guns don't kick too much, and can send a charge exactly where you point them. The ideal pheasant gun is worth enough to be proud of but not too much to worry about. It fits tight, feels balanced, and always seems to find the sweet spot in your shoulder. You'll know you've found the right pheasant gun when you hate to put it down and make regular trips to the gun cabinet to be sure there's no sign of rust forming on it.

The best hunting companions pardon your dog's sins and even manage to find a trait in the canine worth complimenting. My friends, for instance, are forever amazed by my setter's ability to run nearly as fast as a pheasant can fly. The most enjoyable comrades share your reverence for ringnecks and always remember to bring an extra box of 6s because they know you'll forget them about a third of the time. People who hunt pheasants share an affinity for the simple pleasures in life, and there is added harmony when wandering farm country with others who appreciate the beauty of wide fencerows, and who understand what a field of grass means to pheasants, dogs, and memories.

If I could design the perfect pheasant hunting partner, he'd have to be patient, for it invariably takes me an extra ten minutes to stow my gear, and I've been known to forget such items as my shotgun and even my dog. He wouldn't mind stopping at every country store between home and the hunting ground to look for a dusty box of paper cartridges or an old shotgun for sale behind the counter. He'd have to be roughly my size so that when my side-by-side doesn't fire both barrels, his extra gun would fit me comfortably. He'd also have to like hunting at sunrise before the frost has melted off the cover. He'd pack an extra cheddar sandwich on whole-grain bread and a crisp McIntosh for lunch. He'd volunteer to drive and would send the landowners who let us hunt on their properties a gift at Christmas—signing both our names.

I have a few soul mates who are as eccentric as I am. We've shared enough hunts to know what to expect from each other and our dogs. Phil will hunt at a moment's notice and spends his annual vacation allotment between October 1 and November 30. Keith can get access to property that's been posted for so long that others have given up asking. Gary is to a pheasant what a fox is to a mouse; his prowess at locating ringnecks borders on the supernatural.

Phil became a wingshooter by association. I introduced him to Thor, and the sage dog did the rest. An afternoon of shooting over a quality pointing dog will sometimes convince even ardent waterfowlers to turn an eye toward the uplands. Phil became enamored by the savvy dog and at my prompting purchased a setter pup of his own—probably before fully realizing what a handful the energetic breed can be. Despite that, we still speak.

Keith was heir apparent to a corn-rimmed marsh that was seemingly a small slice of Iowa's best pheasant country misplaced in southern Wisconsin. From his hilltop homestead, cackling pheasants could be heard across the expanse of sedges and cattails. The best way to separate pheasant from marsh was with the help of Thor, and thus the basis of our symbiotic relationship was formed. I needed Keith for his prime hunting locale, and he needed me for my dog.

When Gary heads into pheasant habitat, he seldom leaves it without a rooster tail or two protruding from his game vest. He slinks like a predator through cover and somehow manages to find the precise location of the only birds in a hundred-acre field. He's the rare hunter who seems capable of thinking like a pheasant. Perhaps that's the secret after all, for pheasant country is as much a state of mind as it is a place. If we stray too far from such a place, we have only to look into the past to find it again.

STEVE GROOMS

Steve Grooms first hunted pheasants around his home in central Iowa in 1955. When he went to college, Grooms kept a shotgun in the closet of the dean's office so he could hunt pheasants in stolen moments between classes.

"Field Trips" is a true story. Improbably enough, the events all took place exactly as described. The only liberty the author has taken is writing in the first person voice although the man who created and experienced the field trips is his friend, Dick McCabe. McCabe, a superb story-teller in his own right, generously authorized Grooms to present his story in print here.

Grooms is a freelance writer whose books include Modern Pheasant Hunting, Pheasant Hunter's Harvest, The Cry of the Sandhill Crane, The Ones That Got Away, The Return of the Wolf, *and* The Complete Pheasant Cookbook.

nine

FIELD TRIPS

by Steve Grooms

want to say right at the start that this was the
goofiest scheme I've ever hatched. My plan was
to teach a hunter education class to some
mentally disturbed teenagers from the slums
of Chicago. These were kids who had never
hunted, who weren't likely to hunt, and who
were so psychotic they probably shouldn't go
near a loaded gun anyway. So you can see just
how crucial a hunter education class would be
for their development. But it's funny how things
turn out. The class produced the two most fantastic pheasant seasons of my life, and gave the
kids memories too precious to be measured.

This all happened in the mid-1960s.
That was the peak of the Soil Bank era, a time
when northern Iowa was absolutely stiff with
pheasants. If you drove any of the gravel roads
around the little town of Waverly, which is

where I was living and going to college, you wouldn't need an hour to count a hundred pheasants. Pheasants were everywhere. Pheasants ambled into town to eat the stray seeds below bird feeders. Glossy roosters strutted through barnyards, lording it over the domestic roosters. Pheasants darted across blacktop highways, forcing cars into evasive maneuvers that sometimes ended unhappily in the ditches. While walking to class,I even saw pheasants occasionally along a weedy railway track running right by the campus.

Those were grim years for me, in many ways. I was putting myself through college while supporting a wife and two children. Between the demands of a full load of classes and the time required by my job, I was working about seventy hours a week. I barely found enough minutes in a day to grab a sandwich, let alone be a decent father or husband. What did bother me was having no opportunity to go pheasant hunting. So many pheasants; so little time!

For a journalism major whose hobbies were hunting and reading, I had a strange job. I was a "residential psychiatric aide," a fancy phrase meaning I was a dormitory houseparent in a school for screwed-up teenaged boys. I might have been a better psychiatric aide if I had been trained for it, but maybe not. The main requirements were a sense of humor and an instinct for when to duck.

The school existed because society needed a place to stick some flaky and disruptive youngsters who didn't fit anywhere else. In the two years I worked there, I never saw any evidence the school had a clue about how to make sick kids well again. The school hired me as a staff member despite my having zero professional qualifications, which should tell you something.

The kids were referred to our school by courts, mostly from Cook County, which of course is Chicago. In age, they ranged from twelve to sixteen years, and they came in all shapes, colors, and sizes. These kids had gotten crosswise with the law for such things as fighting, stealing, running away, and setting fires. There were no rapists or ax murderers among them, yet each kid came to us with a unique set of bad habits, disabilities, raging hormones, and mental tics. If you caught one of these kids on a good day he might strike you as obnoxious, hyperactive, and obscene—in other words, pretty much your average American adolescent male. But these kids didn't have that many good days. Many of them were inclined to explode in fits of rage that kept my life a lot more interesting than I wanted it to be.

Somebody asked me recently if the kids had been abused, and I had to stop to think. I'm sure they had, but the school's staff never talked that way back then. Today's sensitivity to child abuse hadn't yet emerged. The abuse we worried about was the abuse these kids kept dishing out on us, each other, and on anybody else within arm's reach. The staff kept many of our charges highly medicated with Thorazine and a bunch of other drugs ending in "zine." I often wondered if the doctors dispensing those chemical cocktails knew or cared about the side effects.

For these kids, being shipped to northern Iowa was like being exiled to the dark side of the moon. Remember, these were teenagers from the mean streets of Chicago, where life was fast, violent, and loud. They had never dreamed a place like Iowa existed—a place where everybody talked slow like a record played at the wrong speed, where conversation centered on The Weather, and where the radio stations' notion of soul music was Perry Como crooning "Ave Maria." Many of the kids were astonished to discover cows were real animals. When they learned exactly where milk came from, several got queasy and swore off the stuff. The infinite miles of cornfields surrounding Waverly were alien and terrifying to kids who had routinely played in alleys I wouldn't have entered for a thousand bucks. The staff never worried about our clients running away because the kids felt at home in the school, whereas Iowa seemed weird and spooky.

Desperation is the mother of invention, and I was desperate to go pheasant hunting. That's why I volunteered to teach the hunter education class. Ostensibly, the course would offer the kids some healthy outdoor exercise while instilling mental discipline. A little pheasant boot camp, if you will. Of course I knew these urban urchins needed instruction in the ethics and techniques of hunting about as much as they needed more bad habits. But I wasn't going to let honesty interfere with my chance to chase pheasants during hours I could charge to the school.

Trying to keep a straight face, I gave the school's executive director a dozen reasons why we absolutely had to have a hunter education course. He went ballistic when he heard I meant to take field trips, even though I promised the kids would never lay a finger on a loaded gun. His nightmare scenario was that I would aim low and pepper the butt of a kid who would turn out to have litigious parents. That would jack up our insurance rates and put the school out of business. But even the director could see the course would get the kids' minds off sex for a few minutes and let them blow off energy in God's own clean air.

Moreover, as I pointed out about two hundred times, the class would cost the school nothing.

I finally got a halfhearted endorsement to run a trial course. Nine kids signed up. God only knows what they were expecting. I sure didn't know.

Nobody—*nobody*—was prepared for the way my students responded to the hunting course. Remember, these were kids with the attention spans of gerbils. The drugged ones shuffled around with glassy eyes, and the kids who weren't doped up weren't exactly mental giants. It would be fair to say that the staff had modest expectations for these kids. We were delighted whenever we got them through lunch without a food fight. Our aspirations never included such quixotic goals as actually teaching them anything.

But right from the first day, my course seemed to be the most important thing in the lives of these kids. Hyperactive brats who had never been enthusiastic about anything except setting fire to wastebaskets suddenly focused their minds on a single topic for a solid hour. They took notes. They behaved in and after class. They started calling me "Sir."

It's hard to say why they liked my class so much. I think the kids found the topic unbelievably exotic. Here I was showing them the parts of a gun and how to handle guns safely. While the kids had always been fascinated by firearms, it had never occurred to them that there is a right and legal way to deal with guns. Hunting itself seemed like a legitimized form of killing, which they found mind-boggling. Taking a class about guns and killing seemed something like getting academic credit for learning to hot-wire a car.

It wasn't a fluffy, Hostess Twinkie course. In addition to guns and gun safety, I taught them most of what I knew about ecology, wildlife management, and hunting tactics. I threw a lot of serious stuff at them, including some science, but they kept paying attention and taking notes. Some of them even started going to the library to do outside reading. The staff talked that over and agreed that in the entire history of the school, no kid had entered the library under his own volition. The success of my course wasn't so much surprising as it was astonishing and utterly confounding.

At the end of the course, I gave them a test to see if anything had sunk in. They aced that test—just blew it away. I realized I must have goofed by lowballing the questions, so I wrote a much tougher test. They aced that one too. Everyone on the staff was taking about this phenomenon. All the kids who hadn't signed up for my class were murderously jealous of those who had.

I went to the executive director and showed him both sets of tests. I argued that by doing so well the kids had earned a few field trips. He was still terrified about accidents—not because the kids might get shot, but because the school would suffer were that to happen. But those test scores proved something amazing had taken place. I finally persuaded him with buckets of oozy groveling. My most eloquent argument was something like, "I'll be really, really, really, *really* careful!"

We were the damnedest hunting party ever seen in northern Iowa. The kids didn't own any hunting garb, so they hunted in clothes from the ghettoes of Chicago: gang jackets, Chuck Taylor sneakers, and blue jeans. Back then few stores sold blaze-orange hats, so I required my crew to wear something red on their heads for safety. Some kids wrapped red kerchiefs around their skulls in the fashion of pirates. Others folded bandannas over their noses like the desperadoes in B movies. I would have preferred hunting with just two or three of my students at a time, but any kid left behind would have rioted and trashed the dorm, so I had no choice but to go afield with the whole crazy crew.

We scared the bejesus out of some farmers when we pulled into their yards. Sweet old Scandinavian farmers who had never seen a "negro" in person were suddenly confronted with a van packed with manic youngsters, including several African Americans, dressed like Bluebeard and Jesse James. The kids were so hyped about hunting they looked about ready to chew through the van's windows to get at a pheasant. Many farmers blanched and asked us to leave, but a few were too kind or embarrassed to turn us down.

I learned the only way to hunt pheasants with nine little rowdies is to run drives. We mostly hunted low corn because that way I could keep an eye on everyone in the formation. Herbicides weren't quite as deadly efficient in 1964 as they are now, so many cornfields had enough weeds to be decent pheasant habitat. I had the kids form a line about five yards behind me and the gun. For safety's sake, I insisted they march in a perfect line. It about broke my heart to see how hard the kids tried to be orderly. They would sooner have slit their wrists than screw up and get dropped from the hunting party.

It was an amazing hunt. The kids took on the role of dogs, flushing dogs, although I got one or two points out of them in two seasons. They became insanely competitive about which kid could send the most pheasants flying toward me. After a little experience with pheasants, the kids learned to stomp the weedy spots where roosters like to hide. I taught them to rush the fence at the end of the field and close the formation up to boost pheasants my way. And they got *good*. The kids hunted their hearts out and did their best to give me good shots. That is more than I can say of many dogs with fancier pedigrees and better training.

Things really got funny after I shot a bird. The kids would rush up to me like a squad of Labradors and hold there, absolutely quivering with tension, until I released them. Then nine youngsters would converge on the spot of the fall. There would be a hellacious ruckus featuring lusty swearing, and corn stalks would go sailing in every direction. I would stand back a bit with my shotgun action open for safety, just doubled up in laughter because the kids were such an amazing sight as they dug for a bird. I didn't lose one pheasant in two years. A few birds, however, got stretched or denuded when nine kids tried to retrieve one rooster at the same time.

People sometimes ask me how a juvenile delinquent works out as a hunting dog. The answer is, surprisingly good. When a line of nine hooting, hyperactive youngsters sweeps a field, that field is *swept*. The coolest pheasant on earth doesn't have enough nerve to sit through something like that. The kids' poor sense of smell should have limited their effectiveness, but I swear nine social misfits will outproduce one good springer spaniel any day.

The kids had some unanticipated limitations. I was jolted to learn that several of my little flushers were seriously gun-shy. The first few times I shot at a rooster I'd look around and see two or three kids flat on their tummies. I guess I should have expected that. After all, most of these kids had previous experiences with guns from the streets. When they heard a gunshot, they had been trained to hit the deck.We got around that by having the gun-shy ones walk the outside of the drive line, farthest from the gun. Most kids wanted to walk right next to me because that's where the hottest action was.

I also didn't expect my human retrievers to be terrified by wounded pheasants. If a cock went down dead, they always got it. But if a bird flopped around or took off running, the kids recoiled in horror. That surprised me because these were tough kids from tough neighborhoods. I finally decided the kids visualized violence in some cockeyed, romantic way. They had known guns could kill people, but that knowledge was remarkably theoretical. What had never occurred to them was the fact guns cause *pain.*

We had a few mishaps, although nothing like the ones that terrified the executive director. No kid got his butt tattooed with bird shot.

David was one of my gun-shy kids, a chubby little goofus who was so dim the other kids picked on him all the time. One day we had just lined up for a drive when I saw David's head going away from us down the corn row, running faster than I thought David could go. I didn't know why David had broken rank, but I told the others to step it up. Pretty soon the whole phalanx was trotting along to triple-time speed. Then David's head spun around and came zigzagging back at us as fast as he could go.

David, we learned, had spied an odd animal in the corn and had decided to catch it with his hands. After retreating for a few yards, the skunk got disgusted and gave David a full shot in the face. Perhaps you are wondering why David would decide to pick up a wild skunk with his hands, but if you knew David you wouldn't ask a question like that. That is exactly the sort of decision David specialized in. In the field of poor judgment, David was a towering figure.

One day after we had been out hunting for a while I could tell there was something wrong. The kids were as jumpy as a sack full of weasels and they kept looking at me out of the corners of their eyes. I called a halt and we had a little conference to discover what in the hell was going on.

Finally someone mumbled, "Ummm, Sir, don't get mad, but we sorta lost George."

"*Lost George?*" I quickly counted noses. Sure enough, George's wasn't among them.

"So where is George?"

The kids stared at the toes of their sneakers with hang-dog expressions.

"You know that fence? Well, George is back there. He got hisself stuck."

The only fence I remembered was a wobbly barbed-wire thing that we'd crossed almost half an hour ago. These kids had been blamed for so many things in their lives that they instinctively felt it was their fault when George entwined himself in the wire. They were afraid I'd cancel the field trips when I learned George had screwed up.

We backtracked to the fence. Sure enough, there was George, hung up in the wire like a deer that has made a clumsy jump. He'd managed to run his foot down through a couple strands, then he fell backward and put a twist in the wires. Now he was lying on his back upside down, staring glumly up at the trapped foot. George could have worked himself free except one of the kids had told him the fence might be electrified, so he'd been afraid to touch any wires. If we hadn't finally gone back, George would be there in that fence today.

Our third mishap occurred after we were back safe in the dorms. I decided to teach my class the proper and respectful way to treat game after a hunt. I told the kids an ethical hunter never wastes the meat he has harvested. We all went down to the basement of the dorm where there was a laundry room. The room was too warm and fetid to be comfortable, but it was handy for cleaning birds because it had big sinks and a water supply. I set about demonstrating how to disassemble a pheasant.

Every kid in the room was transfixed. They formed a loose circle around me. As I cut the wings and tails off my first rooster, the kids skooched in tighter, their eyes bugging. I began ripping patches of skin from the bird. The circle of faces pulled in tight until we were like a covey of quail balled up on a cold night. I chopped off the head. The room went absolutely silent. You could have hear an ant sneeze.

Then I said, "If you haven't done this in the field, you'll want to gut the bird now." It didn't occur to me that none of these kids had seen the inside of an animal. Students in rich suburban schools get to dissect fetal pigs in science class, but my students hadn't had a science class with a lab. They were what you might call virgins when it came to the direct experience of intestines.

I slit the belly. The kids had been breathing in and out in unison like one animal. Now they strained forward and quit breathing altogether. I flexed the bird, and a shiny pile of blue-and-pink intestines tumbled out.

Most Americans didn't learn what "projectile vomiting" was until Linda Blair taught them in *The Exorcist* in 1973; lucky me, I got to learn nine years earlier, thanks to David, the intrepid hunter of skunks. David had been facing me, not more than three feet away, when he began spraying his lunch all over his classmates, the naked pheasant, and me.

David's eruption provoked a chain reaction. Almost like a switch had been flipped, half the kids began hurling. Since the kids had been carefully cultivating a macho attitude throughout the course, they were now furiously embarrassed by being sick. So every kid in the room turned and began to thump on David, their favorite scapegoat, even while some of them continued shooting their last meal all over him and the walls.

Rescuing David might have been tricky, but I had the good fortune of being armed with an effective weapon. Swinging the half-gutted pheasant like a broadsword, I laid into the swarm of kids and order was quickly restored. It was a notable moment in the history of science education.

Perhaps I should say more about how good the hunting was. The action was almost nonstop and very noisy. The kids fought all the time about who was going to get the next flush or retrieve. Pheasants often got up in waves, which would cause the kids to howl like civil defense sirens. Some kids got so excited they peed themselves—and no, I am not speaking figuratively. I'm not sure we ever came back with less than a limit of three roosters. Maybe once. And we did most of our hunting late in the season.

When we pushed several birds into the air at once, which we often did, the clamor was apocalyptic. On top of the thunder of pheasant wings there would be the metallic cackles of outraged roosters, the compound roar of nine kids screaming, "That bastard's MINE!" and the BOOM-whickita-BOOM-whickita-BOOM! of my old pump as it barked and kicked out shells.

Our prettiest hunt might have been that morning deep in December right after a storm had whipped through the northern tier of counties in Iowa. That was the only time we hunted a marsh instead of corn. A week of sub-zero temperatures had frozen the marsh as tight as a hockey rink. All the pheasants were tucked down by the base of cattails under about six inches of soft new snow that glinted in the sunlight like a bazillion little mirrors. The air was bitter cold but windless, so the kids huffed out fat clouds of steam as they chugged along like nine little engines that could. When my flying squad of rowdies hit that frozen marsh, roosters began bursting up like popcorn. The old pump went into one protracted spasm of racket, and then nine grinning kids were retrieving three roosters all at once.

Those were the two happiest pheasant seasons of my life. I swear that any moment I wasn't actually shooting birds I was laughing hysterically because the kids were so funny, so earnest, so happy. Even those kids who shuffled through the rest of their time in a drugged haze got swept up in the joy of the hunt. I could hardly believe they were the same youngsters I saw floating through the halls of the dorm.

The field trips became an us-versus-them thing…in other words, our little conspiracy against the school. That gave our hunts, which were already the most exotic thing the kids had done, the heady allure of stolen pleasures. About the only thing more glorious than the face of a happy kid is the face of a happy kid who thinks he's getting away with something.

The kids were thrilled to escape the paternalism and brainless bureaucracy of the school. Beyond that, they knew my butt was on the line with the director. They knew I was trusting them to do the right thing in a setting where screw-ups would be easy and catastrophic. Kids who couldn't meet society's minimum expectations for acceptable conduct were determined to be *perfect* in my presence because they didn't want to give the school an excuse to cancel the field trips. For most of the kids, I was the first grown-up to offer them a significant amount of trust. And they honored that trust, every single one of them.

I try not to think about what happened to those kids after they finally packed up their belongings and returned to the fast times and dysfunctional families they'd left in the slums. I fear life for most of them was at least as chaotic and painful after their stay at the school as it had been before. I did hear that one of my kids came to terms with his private demons, got a job, and actually became a pheasant hunter. But he was the exception. Several of our kids eventually went to prison, which was more the usual case.

My bizarre field trips, invented for purely selfish reasons, probably gave many of my kids the most unalloyed moment of happiness they ever knew. Their lives were like black-and-white movies, gritty and grainy, into which a capricious editor splices a snippet of Technicolor. Unfortunately, that color segment was pathetically brief and absurdly out of context with the rest of the film. But I believe the kids appreciated that fleeting moment of radiant color as much as they had exulted at the sight of roosters surging out of corn into the cold winter sky.

RANDY LAWRENCE

Randy Lawrence spent thirteen years teaching English and coaching football in the public schools before becoming a teacher of writing at Hocking College in Nelsonville, Ohio. Before, after, and sometimes in between classes, he chases pheasants with his Longhunter English setters and pointers in coverts close to home. Randy freelances with a number of wingshooting/bird dog publications and is a field editor for Sporting Clays Magazine. "Home to Roost" is his second work of fiction for Countrysport Press.

ten

HOME TO ROOST

by Randy Lawrence

He told the story to only one person, but that person was my grandmother. Whenever we were alone after he died, she'd tell me about Granddad Converse and the roosting pheasants.

"He and your Uncle LeMoyne hadn't done so good that year. They were workin' at the foundry in town and farmin', too, so there wasn't much time for huntin'. And those boys dearly loved noodles and pheasant dumplings." Her dried-apple face would crinkle a grin, and she'd already be giggling when she got to the part where Granddad and his younger brother were slipping out of the Model A at twilight, planning their assault on the sprawling oak that stood a quarter mile behind a neighbor's farmhouse.

"Your granddad said they could see the birds roostin', that tree just huddled thick with 'em, all black and big and still. He always claimed LeMoyne shot first, but I figure Earnest did. LeMoyne never did anything first when they were together."

Grandma's shoulders would be shaking as she tried to finish her story, laughing into tears of mirth, fumbling for the handkerchief she kept tucked into the belt of her shapeless, floral-print dresses. "Anyhow, there were two shots, all this flappin' and squawkin' commotion, and three birds came tumbling out of that tree. Your granddad ran to gather the one nearest to him and was turnin' for the car when he looked down to see he'd shot into Junior Deeds' barred rock chickens!"

Intention to break game laws was bad enough; shooting another person's poultry was heinous. A week later, my grandfather crept to the Deeds' back porch after midnight with an anonymous payment: one case of canned produce and two of my grandmother's young turkeys, freshly killed, immaculately dressed.

Over on the east side of the county, where I was raised in the generous shadow of my other grandfather, we had a few pheasants, though as a child I never saw one alive. Sometimes city friends who did business at our farm market would come to hunt them, stopping later on the store's front porch to show us a bird or two, and usually three or four rabbits.

One man gave Grandpa Lawrence the vainglorious head of a ringneck, and Grandpa mounted it on a green-and-gold autumn gourd that he thought was somewhat pheasant-shaped. He called his creation "Cornucopia" and brought it over to us kids after the market closed for the night.

My mother was appalled. I smuggled the thing into my bedroom and secreted it under my bed where Mom found it the following spring, her broom dredging out dust bunnies, bubble gum wrappers, and that molding pheasant head on a sagged-in, rotted gourd. My sister heard her scream from where we were playing in the back yard, and Grandpa and I both had to lie low for a while after that one.

There are other pheasant stories from my childhood: of Great-uncle George, the Florida snowbird who surfaced at reunions to return grace before dinner, riding the fenders of shock-sprung jalopies through harvested South Dakota grain fields, potting pheasants on the move; of mongrel farm collies who flushed and fetched "better'n any full-blooded bird dog"; of Trooper, my cousin John's pointer, shot dead on that first pheasant hunt after his master returned home from the Philippines in 1946, a soon-to-be-ex-friend swinging on a rabbit just as the white dog cast back across the front.

My own first pheasant, the one I took with Weird, I could never talk about.

Greg Beard was a senior football co-captain, rugged enough to make the all-conference team as a 135-pound linebacker. I was a junior, playing only on the bomb squads, chasing down kicks and punts. My life was arranged around trying very hard to prove myself worthy of running with the Big Dogs.

Greg was really only a fringe Big Dog. His nickname among the seniors was "Weird," and he sported thick, horn-rimmed glasses above a prominent nose and the first mustache any of us managed to grow after the school dress code had been repealed, sort of a flesh-and-blood Groucho getup.

The eyeglasses fogged inside his football helmet, so Weird played half blind, a myopic pit bull slipping blockers, savaging ball carriers. Good as they were, though, Greg's football skills were secondary to his status as Limbo King and Keeper of Black Betty.

Over the summer, Weird, working out of the bed of his dad's El Camino, had liberated a generously sized, incredibly engineered brassiere from the marching band's Featured Twirler. Though a notorious back seat debutante, Featured Twirler had feigned coy reluctance about donating such an artifact until, vowing secrecy, Greg swooned about what memories a keepsake like this would evoke should his frighteningly low lottery number earn him fast passage to the "conflict" still raging in Southeast Asia. Hours later, Greg drove the young woman home, *sans lingerie*; he reported to our early practice the next morning with a new talisman on display in his locker, new tales for his teammates.

Dubbed "Black Betty" by awestruck visitors to Weird's little shrine, the bra became the finishing touch on a ritual we performed before especially important games. Coaches, afraid of what they might have to stop if they stayed, would vacate the field house while a junior tackle we called "Gut" broke out empty trash cans for himself and another guy who played drums in a local garage band. As they pounded out a jungle beat, the seniors would line up while the rest of us roared the "rain chant" from the movie *Woodstock*. One by one, upperclassmen would try to limbo under a push-broom handle stretched between two nervous team managers.

Lower and lower that broom handle would go until, every time, there was only Weird left with a clean pass under the bar. Stripped to a pair of gym shorts, he'd solemnly place Black Betty, cups up, on the concrete floor beneath the broom. Bouncing to the now-hysterical beat of Gut's drum, the rest of us banging the sides of lockers, he'd toe-walk forward, thigh and stomach muscles corded. Just under the bar he would pause, arch back his neck, and seize Black Betty in his teeth before continuing his sinuous slide under the broom. The place would go bonkers, and we were ready to wreak mayhem on the gridiron.

Traveling to away games, Weird always sat alone, brooding, working up a game face. Coming home, I learned that he could stand a little company, that he seemed relieved and didn't want to talk football. He and I would share a seat over the bus wheel-well, ahead of the seniors and just behind the underclassmen, where it was quiet enough to talk about hunting, a shared passion.

As flattered as I was about hanging with a Big Dog, Weird caught me completely off guard when he suggested getting together to hunt pheasants once the football season was over. He wondered if I knew of any place to go.

I wanted to lie and say "yes," just to show I was worthy of the invitation. But the truth was that I had never hunted pheasants; I kicked around for rabbits and squirrels on our home farm, but there were no birds there. After I confessed, Weird thought for a minute, then told me about pheasants on land adjoining his dad's property, how he always saved them for his own hunts, but would make an exception if I wanted to come along.

The Beard family lived in a battered, pea-green house trailer and cash rented their farm. Weird's mom had died when he and his older brother were still in elementary school, and their dad tottered to our football games on leg braces and twin canes, legacy of a horrible truck crash that had killed a man riding with him. Mr. Beard clung to his farm, drawing a disability check and pooling his ground into the thousands of acres chemically cleansed and religiously fall-plowed by a farmer down the road. No place there for pheasants.

But the neighbors' ramshackle sheep operation, with its jungle fencerows and small fields of weedy row crops, harbored ringnecks in numbers. Weird bragged that even a rookie like me could take a limit out of such a pheasant factory.

Two Saturdays after we'd cleaned out our football lockers, I drove my mother's car, the old Buick with a buzzer governor on the speedometer, out to the Beard's trailer. Weird was waiting and, within twenty minutes, I was holding his .22-20-gauge Savage, broken open, while he climbed the fence between his dad's farm and the Seckel place. I handed Weird his gun, then Grandpa Lawrence's crusty looking "Nitro Special" double, and put my green rubber boot into one square of woven wire. In a hurry, I swung my other leg over, caught my toe on the top strand, and flopped over in a heap. I lay there unable to breathe, legs tangled, with half the box of shells I'd dumped into the stiff pocket of my new vest spilled around me.

Face on fire, I waited forever for my breath to return, then kicked my way out of the fence. I plucked cartridges from yellow roots of dead poverty grass while Weird looked on in disgust.

"Keee-RISTE, Lawrence, you are one *natural* athlete. We ain't even started yet and already we're waitin' on you!" It was the same sort of woofin' he dished out in football huddles, needling opponents, keeping himself hyped. "Before, I was only worried about you trying to put the moves on one of ol' Seckel's sheep. I didn't know I was gonna have to carry your gun for you, too!"

I managed a devastatingly clever "Eat me" in retort before grabbing my heavy gun and hustling over to one side of our first objective: a long stretch of weeds and cattail clumps that thumbed out of the fencerow, eighty yards into a picked corn field.

Envious of Weird's new combination gun, thinking it the height of small-game utility, I waited until he loaded both the lower shotgun barrel and the upper rifle one before levering open my Lefever and slipping in two shiny brass No. 5s. I was embarrassed about toting such an antique, especially with the rubber kick pad Grandpa had anchored with two galvanized roofing nails. But I knew how it shot on rabbits, knew how to handle it safely, and kept it on red alert as we stalked the strip that had lain wet in the spring, foiling the Seckel's corn planter. I watched how easily Weird carried the little Savage and vowed I'd save my chore money and have a "modern" gun before next season.

We worked across the corn field, hit another fence, and took it into a closely cropped woodlot, pasture for a motley band of Hampshire sheep, undocked tails hanging like woolly bowling pins between their back legs. At the place where the woods petered out into a field of bean stubble, Weird stopped to kick at a thigh-high roll of woven wire, rusted and laced with weeds. A rabbit squirted out the back end, bolted for the bean field, then juked back toward the fenceline just as Weird's lower barrel caught up and piled the cottontail, heels over head.

"All *right!*" I yelled as Weird popped open the Savage, let the shell kick back over his arm, and coolly dug for a fresh cartridge.

"Easy shot," he muttered, stooping to lift the rabbit by its back legs, sidling over so I could thread it, headfirst, into the game bag at the back of his brown canvas coat. "Let's go find those damn pheasants. We can hunt rabbits anyplace."

Bare trees behind the Beards' trailer were stabbing at a wan, winter sun by the time we'd covered all but one field of the Seckel farm. We had not moved a single bird, only jumped another rabbit that I missed two feet behind. All afternoon we had been saving a fifteen-acre patch of head-high horseweeds. Three sides bordered picked corn; the fourth, a muddy pond where the sheep came down out of the woods to drink.

From the center of the horseweeds rose a wrecked wooden silo, rusty hoops drooping around split and rotted boards. The skeleton silo marked a graveyard for old machinery parts and the original home site on this land. "If birds're on this farm at all," Weird growled as we trudged to one corner of the weed patch, "here's where they'll be."

"We'll go in this way, stay about twenty yards apart, and weave back and forth, headin' toward the opposite corner. You won't be able to see the fence, but we're headin' west, right into the sun. Take a line off that.

"If we ain't moved nothin' by the time we hit the far corner, we'll split up, hunt the fenceline all the way around, and meet back here. Make sure of what you're shootin' in this tall stuff. No rabbits, no low shots at all. Just pheasants. In the air."

I nodded, chafing at that last admonition, as if I'd ever take a heedless shot, ever *consider* ground-sluicing a game bird. Hmph. Bracing the Lefever against my right thigh, barrels skyward, I parted dry husks of horseweed with my left forearm, and stepped into the field.

Old harrows bared their tines like curled, red claws from matted orchard grass. Cracked tires humped in careless mounds, and a single-row pull-behind corn picker was toppled over on its side like some dead dinosaur. A 1920s-era truck, windows shattered, doors off, squatted on its axles, a cenotaph to the family who had farmed this ground before the Seckels, the ones who had lost their deed in the Depression and moved into town to find other work.

I tripped over the handle of an old lard bucket hidden in the grass, but kept my feet, moving back and forth into the sun and whistling for Weird every minute or so, stopping to listen for his return whistle before moving on. Three times, rabbits bounded off through the trash; the big gun flipped to port arms, then back upright as I circled multiflora rose clumps and a pickup load of gnarled Osage-orange fence posts—short strands of wire still stapled to them—tossed like jackstraws in the weeds.

When I could just make out the corner posts of the fenceline, I heard Weird off to my right. I whistled once, then twice. I was wetting my lips for a third try when the first three birds lifted.

They must have been running ahead of us, scuttling in and out of the farm trash until the cover thinned at the fence. The rattle-clutter of their rise startled me, and I was squinting into the low sun when a dozen more broke out.

There was cackling, and I heard Weird's 20-gauge rap a single time before I could get the Lefever mounted and through the spade-shaped tail banking off to my left. I remember fumbling for the front trigger, but can't recall the shot, only the dark silhouette of that bird, faltering, then folding.

"I got one down!" I whooped, hurdling the slats of an overturned farrowing crate and sprinting to where I'd marked the fall. I was frantically searching, cold panic creeping in at the thought of a lost bird, when I heard Weird shout. He had climbed a stump so I could see him above the weeds, grinning under that Groucho 'stache and glasses. Over his head he dangled a Technicolor November rooster, its bright-white cleric's collar glowing.

Turning back, I bent double, pawing through the grass, before a flash of mottled tan and spread wings caught my eye five yards ahead. I'd found my bird, but I stood staring a long time before reaching down to pick up my first game bird. A hen.

I held her in my hands, wings smoothed against her sides, gorge rising in my throat, when Weird came stomping up. "Can you believe this?" I said, turning, holding the bird out for him to see, then reaching around to stuff her out of sight in my game pouch.

Faster than I could react, a gloved hand swatted the pheasant away. "For crissakes, don't pick it up!" Weird spat. Shouldering me to one side, he kicked the limp brown form further into high weeds screening a pile of twisted pipe. "It's 'possession' if you've got it in your hands, you stupid—"

"I'm not leaving that bird," I vowed, voice heating up to match Weird's. "I screwed up, I'll take the blame, but I'm not wasting that pheasant on a fox!" I started for the tall weeds, but Weird barged in front of me, his face eight inches from mine.

He half snarled, half whispered, jabbing his finger into my chest.

"'Wasted' is exactly what you'll be if Emory catches you hen-shootin'. There'll be a fine, for sure, and they might take your license for a year, maybe your gun. One pheasant worth that to you?" Emory Jividen was the game protector, a shirttail relative on my mother's side, and a notorious hard-ass. He would love to bust a cousin, just to prove he played no favorites.

I wanted to cry, wanted to fight, wanted to wrap that old shotgun around a fence post, then spike it into the scrap heap of pipe. Instead, I just stood there, fingering the safety of the Lefever back and forth. Weird kept hammering me.

"We get caught shootin' a hen on Seckel's, that's the last I'll get on their place. Ever! How the hell could you not see that was a hen? There were two, maybe three, roosters out your side, and you pick a hen to shoot! How did you manage that?"

I'd played enough football for a former-Marine head coach to recognize this line of questioning. I swallowed something about looking into the sun and being overanxious, and maybe just the plain fact that I'd never before even seen a pheasant when I'd had a gun in my hand. But I knew better than to say those things. Each was a reason; none was a good excuse. This wasn't like Granddad's deal at the roost—the only witness a fellow perpetrator, penance to be left on a moonlit back porch. I kept still and took my medicine.

Weird let up by the time we made the half mile back to the property line fence, and we walked silently through his barnyard. Mr. Beard saw us from the window, and hobbled out the trailer door. "I heard you shootin'," he offered, leaning forward on his canes.

"Got one and missed one, Dad," the rabbit forgotten in pheasant pride. Weird contorted himself around and tugged the cock bird from his coat. It popped out backward, body feathers disheveled, the long tail broken.

"Rabbit, too." He shifted the bird to his gun hand, twisted back into his coat, and worked free the stiff, fur-mussed cottontail. I stayed off to the side, gun broken over my shoulder, working at my most rueful should-have-had-more-but-I-can't-shoot-worth-crap smile.

"Clean 'em in the barn, Greggie, then you boys come in and tell me about your hunt." Mr. Beard poled himself around, managed the door, and stumped inside.

Weird came back, the pheasant and rabbit held behind him. "I'll tell him you got chores at home," he said, his voice flat. "I'll just clean this bird, hang him for another couple days, pluck him maybe Tuesday." He looked away toward the barn. "They gotta hang at least a couple days to be any good at all. The rabbits, Dad likes to put in saltwater overnight. Soaks the wild out of them."

I started to say how sorry I was, but could only cough up, "Hey, that's fine, thanks for the hunt. I'll see you on Monday." Weird was almost to the barn before I turned for my car...

Eighteen years later, it is a remarkably cool summer's evening on another farm at the county's east end. I have just hazed a tired setter puppy back into her kennel. After hosing out the green slime, I fill her rubber bucket with fresh water, then step away to watch the pup drink, black-speckled head chopping at the water.

A half hour before, we found a flock of young pheasants in the overgrown orchard. In the part nearest the oats stubble field, they held well for the young dog, though after the first two solid points, she ran up the rest of them, yipping at the ones that flushed right off the end of her nose. Only when the last bird clattered over the fence did she come back and flop at my feet, sides heaving, tongue lolling.

It took college, then ten years teaching in a high school and coaching football before I picked up a gun and went looking for pheasants again. By then, I'd bought a run-down 180 acres with money my dad's dad left me. My wife and I propped up the barn, ran chainlink and cement kennels out one end, and are living in a rented double-wide until the new house gets built.

Our carpenters are also my neighbors, Amish farmers who tolerate fencerows, spill grain from antique harvest equipment, make do without chemicals, plow behind stolid Belgian horses in the spring. Between my place and my neighbors', we have pheasants.

The Amish work my ground on the shares, at my direction: first-cutting alfalfa, brome, and timothy, hayed late to protect brooding hens. The outside four rows of corn and beans are left standing for feed in the fall. Behind the barn we grow an acre of sunflowers. Pheasants are there on gray, winter days, their beaks battering at the bowed seed heads like boxers at a speed bag.

At the far corner of the sunflower patch is a blown-over hickory. One snowy morning this past January, my early walk turned up five cock birds, bright as Christmas ornaments, perched in its branches.

I have tried paying for that first hen many times over, counting every bird in hand against the many we've provided for in the bush. Even then, I know I can never quite make good. But I can get better.

Just as Granddad learned a lesson about greed at the roost, I have found that whenever I try to impress another person in the hunting field, the day will go wrong. Guaranteed. For a long time, I hunted alone, unable to trust myself, then later, with Arran, the patch-eyed dam of that black-and-white puppy.

Arran has taught me to be keen, but honest, even a bit overawed, in the presence of game. I have seen her haughty frame broken down in a rage of pheasant scent, grotesque poses that almost frighten me as I circle the stand, working to get her bird to fly. There is wing flurry, sometimes an oath of cackling, then gunfire that seems distant, detached. Occasionally an impossibly long, parti-colored bundle is ferried in by a soft setter mouth, offered like a gift.

However it goes, we return each night having once more tried to prove something about being worthy, but now only to ourselves: either we hunted hard and hunted well, or cut corners, got lazy, took advantage. Sleep will either come easily, or drag behind as we fidget and toss, learning to live with what we've brought home to roost.

JIM FERGUS

Jim Fergus is a freelance writer whose work has appeared in a variety of magazines and newpapers, including Newsweek, Newsday, Esquire, Outside, The Paris Review, Fly Fisherman, Harrowsmith Country Life, The Denver Post, The Dallas Times-Herald, *and others. He is a field editor of* Outdoor Life *magazine, for which he writes a monthly column, "The Sporting Road." His book,* A Hunter's Road: A Journey with Gun and Dog Across the American Uplands, *was published in 1992 by Henry Holt and Company, and recently went into its fourth hardcover printing.*

Currently Fergus is completing a Natural History Guide to Rocky Mountain National Park *for Houghton-Mifflin Company, as well as a collection of novellas about the Northern Cheyenne Indians. The research for the latter conveniently took him across five prime pheasant and prairie-grouse states during bird season. He plans to hit the road again this fall with his yellow Lab, Sweetz, to research the sequel to* A Hunter's Road, *titled* A Hunter's Season.

eleven

THE PHEASANT QUEST

by Jim Fergus

ver one-third of the world's (48) pheasant species are endangered—partly through killing, but especially as the result of the loss of habitat.

John P. S. Mackenzie
Birds of the World: Game Birds

Sweetz and I were stalking the wily Lady Amherst pheasant (*Chrysolophus amherstiae*) in its native land—the high mountains of eastern Tibet. It is as preposterous looking a bird as its name implies, only slightly less so than its close cousin the golden pheasant (*Chrysolophus pictus*), which we would hunt the following month in central China, and which, with its coifed swept-back blond head, bright red belly plumage, and over-the-top thirty-inch tail, looks terrifyingly like Dudley Dooright in drag. Frankly, as I was soon to discover, it can be embarrassing even to hunt such a bird. In the case of the Lady Amherst, you must be doubly discreet at cocktail parties regarding any boasting about your hunting exploits. The most casual remark, such as "I bagged a lovely brace of Lady Amhersts today," can be a real conversation stopper.

I had already killed a thirty-five pound wild common peafowl (*Pavo cristatus*) on the wing in Sri Lanka at the beginning of our impossible journey. I specify "on the wing" because if you've ever seen a domesticated peafowl (or peacock, as, of course, the better-dressed male is called), which are sometimes raised as ornamental birds on farms and private estates, you might be under the mistaken notion that such an enormous bird cannot fly. Not so. Given a good running start—which can be readily attained after a fifty-yard foot race with a pursuing yellow Lab—the peafowl, once launched and airborne, is a fast and dexterous flyer, swooping through the trees much like a ruffed grouse. And when you kill one in such a situation they come down so hard that it's a lot like a single-engine plane crash; I've seen them snap full-grown trees in half like toothpicks. As big as they are, however, peafowl can be plenty challenging to shoot. If you've ever misjudged your lead due to the deceptively long tail of our own ringneck, wait'll you see the peacock's ludicrous plumes trailing five feet behind. Then there's the matter of cleaning the damn things—what to do with all those feathers?…But wait a minute, I'm getting way ahead of myself now.

My dog, Sweetz, and I were on an odyssey of sorts—a five-month tour of Asia and Indochina to hunt all the known species of pheasants in their native habitats for a book we were working on, tentatively titled, *The Pheasant Quest: In Search of the Mythic Ditch Parrots of the Old World—with Gun, Dog, and a Sherpa Named Sabu*…or, *Sweetzer does Asia*.

On our list were such exotic species as the Himalayan Monal pheasant (*Lophophorus impejanus*) which we would hunt shortly in the mountains of Nepal; from there into neighboring Sikkim and Bhutan after the elusive Satyr Tragopan (*Tragopan satyra*). And we still had the Elliot's pheasant (*Syrmaticuls ellioti*) to go, in the mountains of the Chekiang and Fukien provinces in southeastern China;

and from there a long hazardous overland trip into central China for the aforementioned golden pheasant; and the Reeves pheasant (*Syrmaticus reevessi*) in Chinese hill country; and then the stunning silver pheasant (*Lophura nycthemerus*) in China's Kunlun mountains, after which we would make an even more brutal trek that involved crossing the Gobi desert to reach the mountain country of Mongolia for the Pallas' snow, or blue-eared, pheasant (*Crossoptilon auritum*)— a handsome blue bird with a long bushy tail like a feather duster. And that's only the beginning. Even more dangerous would be our quest for the Korean ring-necked pheasant (*Phasianus colchicus karpowi*)—a larger variety than its Chinese cousin—which would necessitate a tricky and highly illegal midnight border crossing into

North Korea, for a chapter entitled, "Poaching in Commieland." Bird hunting is many things to all of us, but it so rarely gets a chance to be downright heroic.

I was leaving the travel details entirely to my trusty guide Sabu, who assured me with a tiny inscrutable Sherpa smile, that he "knew some people." We had a lot of ground to cover, but if there was time, and assuming we survived the Korean adventure, we planned to make a sea passage to the Malay Peninsula to hunt the great argus pheasant (*Argusianus argus*)—a huge jungle species.

Some years ago the government of China concluded that birds were having a negative effect on agriculture. Millions of people were sent into the fields and what is left of the forests to beat pans in order to frighten the birds. This was kept up for days until huge numbers died of exhaustion and starvation. Thus, by decree, virtually all birds in agricultural areas were eliminated.

John P. S. Mackenzie
Birds of the World: Game Birds

Imagine the spectacle, not to mention the ungodly racket: all those dutiful Chinese citizens banging their pots day in and day out to make their world safe from birds. It's too communist for words, isn't it? Of course it goes without saying that like nearly all such schemes against the natural world, it didn't work. Without birds, insect pests multiplied unchecked and soon the Chinese government was changing their insane policies to encourage bird life.

It can't help but occur to the concerned American sportsman that we have accomplished, albeit in somewhat less dramatic fashion, largely the same goal of eliminating some of our own native game birds from their native ranges. This is why—and I hope you will forgive me for saying this in such a collection and among such august company of pheasant lovers—I am not an enormous fan of our imported Chinese ring-necked pheasant (*Phasianus colchicus*).

This is heresy, I know, but for one thing, due to their starlinglike habits of parasitism, hen pheasants frequently lay their eggs in the nests of other birds, such as, for instance, the prairie chicken, therefore hastening that already precarious species' decline. Don't get me wrong: everything considered, I'm glad pheasants are here and that they so conveniently fit the ecological niche we have made for them in the process of "beating the pots" against our own native game birds. And I hunt them myself every chance I get. But pheasants are, after all, easily domesticated and easily raised commercially, both for food and as targets; at best they're really just fancy chickens gone wild. Given the choice between hunting a prairie chicken on a vast expanse of virgin prairie, and a pheasant in a corn field, I'll take the prairie chicken every time.

As for the driven pheasant shoots that are put on with such pomp and circumstance in Great Britain, though I would agree with the redoubtable Datus Proper that the English make good lunches, I'd frankly just as soon stay home, eat a sandwich, and have someone wing Frisbees over my head.

Such grousing (okay, bad pun) is, of course, largely sentimental. People and stock must have corn to eat, farmers must make a living, and shotgunners must have live, edible targets. Given the way things are going these days for the prairie chicken (both the lesser and greater species), and the way things have already gone for its close eastern cousin the heath hen (extinct since roughly 1932), the pheasant certainly represents a tremendous boon to American sportsmen. The species is, in a genuine sense, the "opiate of the shooting masses." At the same time, organizations like Pheasants Forever are doing an enormously valuable service to all by encouraging farmers to preserve a bit of cover and habitat— fencerows and corners and unmowed borrow pits—and to lay off the pesticides and herbicides as much as possible, so that pheasants not only have something to eat, but also have somewhere decent and healthy to live. I just believe we should extend the same courtesy to our native birds, who, after all, were here first.

Those who shoot pheasants, grouse [sic: grouse cannot be pen raised] *and partridges in Europe and North America now rely to some extent on birds raised in pens and released for the pleasure of the hunters—usually an hour or two before being shot. Pheasants, Gray (or Hungarian) Partridges and Chukars are easily semi-domesticated and can be bred in large numbers. Barring disease, they reproduce well with a high survival rate. One shoot that I know of in Ontario, Canada, raises about 15,000 pheasants each summer.*

John P. S. Mackenzie
Birds of the World: Game Birds

All of my niggling complaints about the introduced Chinese ring-necked pheasant notwithstanding, it is, of course, another thing altogether to hunt truly wild pheasants in their native lands. Even if you never get to make a tour through Asia like the one Sweetz and I have embarked on, it's a fine thing just to know that those birds are there— isn't it?—breeding and living out their remarkable little game bird lives in the wild. And it's fine to know that as long as they are extant in their native lands, we might one day get over there to hunt them. Or not. What truly matters is that once they are gone, they will simply be gone. Forever. And what are our chances of hunting them then—or of even concocting a reasonably plausible fantasy about it? I believe that a little piece of every bird hunter dies with the demise of each species. I still mourn the heath hen and the passenger pigeon, both departed from this earth before I was born.

Maybe it was the thin air up there in the Himalayas of Nepal, or maybe it was the single-malt Scotch whisky Sabu and I were sharing from a flask I carried in my game bag, but these were the thoughts going through my mind after Sabu and Sweetz and I made camp for the night following a successful, if exhausting, day of pheasant hunting. Lying on the ground next to us was a spectacularly beautiful brace of Himalayan Monal cock pheasants which I had just bagged—my first double, needless to say, on Himalayan Monal pheasants, kicked up just at the end of the day by Sweetz and clearly killed by yours truly, first right and then left.

Now Sabu and I sipped our whisky and relived the day's hunt, admiring the birds' stunning plumage. With its iridescent gold-and-blue back, contrasting red tail and exquisite green quail-like topknot, the Himalayan Monal pheasant has been called by one expert "probably the most striking of all birds."

Not only are they handsome, they are a hardy species as well, living as they do up here at the top of the world. Indeed, I wondered why we hadn't tried introducing them to selected mountainous regions of the United States. I mean, look how well chukars have done in certain western states. In fact, it occurred to me that given the endangered status of one-third of the world's forty-eight pheasant species, and the relative ease with which the genus is domesticated and bred in captivity, why aren't we stocking other exotic pheasant species (of which, according to my research, there is one suitable for nearly every conceivable habitat) all over the United States? Imagine climbing the mountains of, say, Colorado to shoot a Lady Amherst pheasant, or hunting the hill country of Texas for the Reeves pheasant. Or better yet, hunting the oak forests of Georgia for the common peafowl—imagine the thunderous flush, the incredible flash of color! Why in no time there would be an active Peafowl Forever chapter...

Anyway, these were the strange, nearly demented thoughts I was thinking, brought on, I'm certain, by the deadly combination of whisky and high altitude, when all of a sudden a group of eco-tourist trekkers from Boulder (I knew this because they all wore matching trekking T-shirts) accompanied by their own Sherpa attendants marched right into our camp. Sweetz, woken abruptly from a deep, post-hunt slumber, howled hysterically with her legs planted stiffly and the hackles on her back raised menacingly, as is her habit in the sudden presence of strangers. Even though she is quite harmless, the trekkers backed off warily, and when they saw my shotgun leaning against a tree and those gorgeous dead birds...well, you'd have thought that we had a couple of fresh human heads mounted on sticks in camp from the looks they gave us. Sabu and the two Sherpas from the other party apparently knew each other; they performed the Sherpa equivalent of the high-five in greeting, then eagerly crouched over my pheasants to make sounds of approbation in their strange guttural tongue. I decided then and there to invite these fine fellows for dinner, because clearly they would appreciate well-prepared Himalayan Monal pheasant. As for the others, I had learned some years earlier not to waste fresh game on those who sneer at the efforts of hunters. Let them eat cake, I say.

Now just as I was having the rather unkind thought that these trekkers who had stumbled into my Himalayan base camp were the sort of folks who elicited in me the almost uncontrollable urge to light up an unfiltered Camel and blow a huge lungful of smoke in their faces, a fit, tan young woman dressed head-to-toe in Patagonia attire stepped forward, apparently the self-appointed spokeswoman for the party.

"Did you kill those beautiful birds?" she demanded to know in a not very polite way, especially considering that her party had walked, uninvited, into my camp, interrupting a most pleasant cocktail hour.

"Why, yes, I did," I admitted proudly. "Made rather a nice double of it, too, if I may say so."

"How could you possibly kill something so beautiful?" she asked. "Why those birds belong in a protected bird sanctuary, where people can see them and admire them." Then, believe it or not, she started weeping softly.

"Yes, well, I'm having them for dinner," I said, "with an amusing little Tibetan cabernet I packed up here. Perhaps you'd like to join me?"

With that the girl started wailing in earnest. "You're going to eat them?" she said. "Beautiful creatures like that? Oh my God!" Then she pointed her finger at me and shrieked: "Criminal! Murderer!"

Maybe it was the altitude. Nevertheless it was a strange thing, I can tell you, to be thus accosted on a mountainside in the Himalayas, in one's own camp to boot. Finally, an earnest young man (I think it must have been her boyfriend), who may have inferred from my dinner invitation that I was trying to hit on his girl, stepped forward and put his arm protectively around her, pulling her back, sobbing, to the safety of the group. "Thank you," he said to me sarcastically, "we eat only pure vegan food."

"Vegan?" I asked, unfamiliar with the term. "Is that the same as vegetarian?"

"Vegan," he said with enormous disdain in his voice, "means no animal products whatsoever—no milk, no cheese, nothing that comes from or contributes to our exploitation of the animal world. And certainly, no birds. We subscribe to the dietary teachings of—"

"That sounds mighty grim," I interrupted. "Personally, I subscribe to the dietary teachings of the great Sitting Bull, who said: 'When the buffalo are gone, we will hunt mice. For we are hunters.' "

That, to sum things up, is a bit how I feel about the ring-necked pheasant. When the prairie grouse are gone, I'll eat pheasants. No, I should say—now that the prairie grouse are mostly gone, I do eat pheasants and am grateful for them, too. Anyway, who's going to complain about a large plot of CRP land at dawn, bordering a corn field and brimming with cackling roosters? Not this hunter. Still, it is not the same as hunting wild birds in their native lands.

Wild birds, wild lands, forever!

Himalayan Monal pheasant, while vaguely similar in taste to our own wild ringnecks, is a much richer, deeper, more complex game bird on the table. It cries out, for instance, for a lusty red rather than a white wine. The following recipe, which makes for a delightful camp meal, was provided by my Sherpa guide, Sabu. Measurements are strictly approximate. The secret to the recipe, of course, lies in obtaining a good Tibetan red wine—or for that matter, any Tibetan red wine. Like I said, Sabu knew some people.

SABU'S HIMALAYAN MONAL PHEASANT IN TIBETAN WINE

2 Himalayan Monal pheasants, cut up

1 carrot, sliced thin

1 celery stalk, sliced thin

1 cup whole wild Himalayan mushrooms
  (a small variety similar to our morels)

10–12 whole cloves wild Himalayan garlic
  (these are often found in the crops of Himalayan
  Monal pheasants)

4 teaspoons wild Himalayan chingzas
  (an herb that also grows wild in the Himalayas,
  similar to our basil—which may be substituted in
  an emergency)

2 cups pheasant stock reduced to a thick essence
  (On our journey, Sabu, renowned among the
  Sherpas for his culinary skills, wisely brought
  along an extra llama just to carry our stock pot
  and other cooking gear. This way we had a
  constant supply of fresh pheasant stock.)

1 cup Tibetan cabernet
  (a Tibetan burgundy will also do nicely)

6 tablespoons butter

Salt and pepper to taste

Breast the birds, and remove thighs and legs, taking care to leave the skin on. Save the carcasses for the stock pot. In a heavy cast-iron skillet, brown the pheasant pieces in butter over medium-high heat. Remove pheasant pieces from the pan and set aside.

Sauté carrots, celery, mushrooms, and garlic cloves, adding additional butter as required. After most of the moisture has cooked out of the mushrooms return thigh and leg pieces to the pan, add wine and enough stock to not quite cover the pheasant pieces. Reduce heat, cover pan partially with a lid so that steam can escape, and simmer for about 15–20 minutes (or slightly longer if you are preparing this at high altitude in the Himalayas).

Return the breasts to the pan, add additional stock as necessary, add the fresh chopped chingzas and cook, uncovered, over medium-high heat for an additional 5–10 minutes, being very careful not to overcook, as the breasts will dry out. Arrange the pheasant pieces on a warm platter, with sauce and vegetables poured over them. If the stock has been sufficiently reduced you shouldn't need to thicken the sauce.

Serve with a nice loaf of fresh Tibetan peasant bread, and a bottle of Tibetan cabernet, a glass of which you will hoist to the secretly envious vegans camped nearby.

Bon appetit!

PS This recipe also works for Kansas ringnecks.

STEVE STALLARD

Steve Stallard is currently the Executive Chef for a three-hotel corporation, and has held prior chef positions at the Taillevent Restaurant in Paris, France, and at the Greenbrier Hotel in White Sulphur Springs, West Virginia.

Steve is an avid fly fisherman and fly tier, collector of fine wines, amateur mycologist and photographer, and a consummate hunter whose travels have taken him far and wide in search of game and a taste of wildness.

twelve

A TASTE OF WILDNESS

by Steve Stallard

The dogs are leashed after hours of work, changing slowly from wrist-dislocating fireballs to somewhat sedate and manageable animals. This is a time to savor. The odor of wet dogs and fresh game lingering inside the vehicle. Shots and points recounted with tired companions—each being graciously honored for his skill. Pheasants stacked neatly in the truck next to the kennels, the spent dogs inside showing no particular interest in the birds on the long drive home.

The end of a hunt always leads me to my second passion, my vocation—the culinary arts. As a kid, I was a hunter first, and like most midwestern hunters I stacked the birds in the icebox, getting to them when the season ended. This often meant they were freezer burned by the time they were unceremoniously flopped into cream-of-mushroom soup simmering in Revere Ware.

Fortunately, my curiosity about food preparation turned into yet another obsession. And my love of cooking became a natural compliment to my hunting and fishing. Preparing and cooking game in a manner that would preserve and enhance its natural flavors became a way of showing reverence and respect for the prey. It became the culmination of my days afield.

Even now, my desire to learn culinary arts has a single purpose: to help me gain a complete understanding of game preparations. This can be an impossible and infinite task. Over the years it has taken me to foreign lands and Michelin-ranked French brigades to American hotels and restaurants—all for long hours of painstaking work and low wages. Meanwhile I dreamt of flushes of pheasants in South Dakota and heavy October flights of northern Michigan woodcock.

Yet from my culinary experiences I have gained not only an appreciation of fine cuisine and wine, but a practicality in game cookery. As a hunter, I understand what other American hunters are faced with in handling game, so I have chosen simplicity over complex menus and classic preparations. Unknowing outfitters and shooting-preserve operators hurrying to clean, process, and freeze fresh game miss critical steps necessary for the proper fabrication, aging, and storage of the meat. This is the American hunter's greatest violation. We must take an approach that is similar to the one taken in Europe, where game is the epitome of haute cuisine—highly regarded, very expensive, and rare.

By contrast, this country's abundance of wild game, along with its availability of firearms and vast tracts of public lands, has made hunting accessible to everyone. Some, however, have lost their reverence and respect for what we harvest, at least in comparison to European standards. It is quite common to hear people speak of pheasant that tastes like chicken, or elk that tastes like beef. Our appreciation of game flavor seems to have been stamped out by our American penchant for blandness, for things processed, things fast. But game, when not allowed to stand on its own, loses its identity and integrity—in the strictest sense of taste, and in a much wider sense as well.

Understanding an animal and its flavor further deepens our appreciation of the hunt. No one is born with a discriminating palate. The ability to recognize subtle flavors must be acquired by continuously challenging our taste sensations. Once this is accomplished, we experience a stronger bond with our sport. What follows are fundamental steps for handling game. Many are deeply rooted in classic cooking and handling techniques; some are new cuisine styles and observations from an American hunter and professional chef.

FIELD CARE

Contrary to age-old habits of "cleaning" game, removing entrails immediately after the kill is not the best way to protect the meat from bacteria and spoilage. If the bird has not been badly damaged by shot, or by a dog, the safest way to protect it from bacteria is to let it cool uneviscerated, whole, and undressed.

Rapid spoilage will begin much quicker if an incision is made and the flesh is exposed than if the bird is left feathered and undressed. This is similar to opening a sealed food package. If the seal is broken, the food must be used quickly. As for temperature (both the internal temperature of the bird and the external temperature of the air), it is very important to allow the bird to cool while hanging by the neck. Keep pheasants under fifty-five degrees Fahrenheit for a maximum of two days, then store them at a cooler, safer temperature of between thirty-six and forty-five degrees Fahrenheit. Don't overstack or carry your buddy's birds in your game bag. Hang your birds as soon as possible. Game straps are excellent, providing both a practical and efficient way to properly cool uneviscerated pheasants.

If your plans include driving any distance, or if you cannot hang your kill, place them side by side or single file, being careful not to stack them. Breast-side up is the best way. This protects the premium part of the meat, and allows the possible intestinal fluids and bile to drain to the back and legs. If you must discard a part because of sourness, it is always better that the legs go rather than the breast meat.

AGING

Next to proper field care, aging is an extremely important key to flavoring and tenderizing pheasants. Wild pheasants have tougher meat than domesticated fowl because of all the running and flying they do in their constant struggle to find food and avoid predation. Thus the key to tenderizing pheasants is to slowly let natural bacteria break down the birds' tough muscle tissue. As I mentioned earlier, this process must be done under refrigeration. Although it sounds unhealthy, it's the same method used in all facets of beef production today. Most beef sold in the market is usually two to three weeks old. Even the finest prime beef will be as tough as shoe leather if eaten two to three days after slaughter. The same is true of game. How many times have you had pheasants that had been cleaned and tossed into the pan on the day of the hunt? More often than not, I would guess. Were they tough? Most likely. I've had breast meat from a just-cleaned old rooster that was like chewing on a cowhide collar.

But I have killed other mature pheasants, shot so the intestinal structure was not leaking into the meat and causing sourness. I have aged those same birds two months in my refrigerator, and they were fork-tender on the legs and thighs, and had marvelous flavor.

On the whole, pheasants can take more aging than other light-meated game birds. A minimum hanging time of ten days at a refrigerated temperature of between thirty-six and forty-five degrees Fahrenheit is the general rule for pheasants. This allows bacteria to work slowly, breaking down connective tissues and giving the bird its intrinsic game flavor.

Of course this technique cannot be applied at all times and under all circumstances. It is very important not to try to age heavily shot birds. The possibility of souring due to a badly ruptured stomach or intestine is great. There is, however, another way to deal with these problems. It's called the wet-aging or bag process, and it has been used for years by the meat industry to reduce moisture loss in aged beef. Dry-aged beef will, after about twenty days or so, have approximately a 30 percent moisture loss. To age meat without precious weight loss, a sealed vacuum bag is used to retain moisture and increase profits. Meanwhile, the slow process of controlled bacteria development takes place.

A similar method can be used to age pheasants in your own refrigerator. Cleaned birds can be packaged in an air-tight, heavy-gauge plastic that resists freezer burn exceptionally well. (Moreover, these bags allow you to stack and store birds in such a way as to avoid the hair-raising scream of an unsuspecting person opening the crisper drawer and finding a three-week-old brace of undrawn pheasants.) There are many vacuum packaging machines available on the market at reasonable prices, and these will significantly increase the freezer life and convenience of aging more than anything I have worked with.

Vacuum packaging also works to freeze birds immediately for aging at a later date. If you are out on a shoot and have harvested several birds, they can be frozen and pulled out a week or so before cooking to give them proper aging. But be careful about broken seals or bloated bags. If air intrudes into the meat, you will have little control over the bacteria growth. Always bag-age pheasants in your refrigerator for six to twelve days at a temperature between thirty-five and forty-five degrees Fahrenheit. When the meat is removed, don't be alarmed by the gaseous odor you encounter upon immediately opening the bag. This is natural, and rinsing the bird in plenty of cold water should eliminate the odor. If it doesn't, use your own judgment. Any shot holes with excessive green darkening and a sour or foul smell should be cut away and discarded.

The normal odor from pheasants aged in this manner should be fruity and gamy, pungent but clean and not lingering. Your nose and eyes are the best judge of this. It may be a new smell if you're used to eating unaged pheasant, but it really identifies the pheasant's character and separates it from domestic fowl.

Once you prepare your first few meals from well-aged birds, the new-found flavor will make all the care and preparation seem well worth the trouble. I now put as much detail into field care and aging as I do in hunting.

As for a preference between the two aging styles, I still use the hanging-in-refrigerator method when I can, but it's not always available. If I am at a preserve shoot away from home, or if heat is a factor and refrigeration is not handy, I field process as best I can and vacuum pack at home, freeze, then age accordingly. Trying to bring home birds feathered and undrawn won't work well if you are in eighty-degree heat and throwing them into the coolers with melted ice sloshing around. I generally hunt where I am able to apply proper handling methods.

PREPARATION FOR COOKING

As I mentioned earlier, plucking a bird after proper aging is the best way to prepare it for cooking. The main reason is that the skin acts as a natural barrier, sealing in the bird's moisture. You will notice that an aged bird will pluck much easier than a freshly killed one. After a week or two in a relatively low-humidity environment such as a refrigerator, a significant amount of drying and shrinkage of the skin occurs while the bird ages undrawn and fully feathered. If you try to pluck a pheasant while it's still warm, its skin still moist, you will surely tear it every time. After the skin has tightened and dried through aging, dry plucking is simple if you pull out the feathers a little at a time.

I always prefer the skin left on, but pheasants can be prepared and aged with the skin off. Generally speaking, cooking techniques with the skin removed are either longer, such as braising in moisture, or much quicker, such as high-heat pan-frying, sautéing, or char-grilling. Because moisture is lost with the removal of the skin, your cooking technique needs to adjust. I like to add fat of some sort to the preparation, such as heavy cream or roux-thickened sauces, and sear the birds, then slowly simmer them (essentially braising them in rich sauce), or sauté them quickly until medium done. (By "medium done" I mean the breast meat, not the leg and thigh. Also, braising involves cooking with liquid, preferably stock or seasoned broth, in a covered container until fork tender.)

The ultimate dining experience is a fully-aged pheasant with the skin on, a bird that has matured well and has been properly roasted to complement the finest old red wine in the cellar. Pheasant should be roasted with legs and thighs on, but if the bird hasn't been properly aged, moisture-cooking techniques should be applied—such as braising or confit (cooking in fat)—to avoid toughness. A roasted bird should be trussed and tied with butcher twine to pull legs, thighs, and breast tightly together so even cooking occurs. The pheasant should then be moderately seasoned. I usually like simple light seasonings that allow the bird's natural flavor to come through.

Salt, pepper, a small amount of thyme, or tarragon are fine. Just prior to roasting, the skin should be loosened from the breast meat, and whole cubed butter should be slid between the meat and skin for added moisture and light browning. Seasonings and herbs should also be added under the skin to prevent them from burning. Salt and pepper should be finely sprinkled on top of the skin. High temperatures are needed for good roasting. I prefer conventional ovens preheated to 475 degrees Fahrenheit. Cook approximately twelve to eighteen minutes until dark golden brown. Baste the bird frequently with pan drippings, letting it rest after roasting until fully cooled. This is crucial to retain the flavor and moisture in the bird. If the roasted bird is carved while still hot, the circulating juices will pour out from any cut surfaces, rendering it dry and chewy. If the roasted bird is allowed to cool completely, the juices and moisture will be retained within the meat.

After the bird has cooled, carve the meat from the bone. Separate the breasts into two pieces and separate the legs and thighs. You should find that part of the meat—such as the breast near the bone, or the thighs next to the pelvis—is undercooked. The boned bird is then reheated at 350 degrees Fahrenheit to medium done and served. Accompaniments and sauces should vary to your tastes.

These following recipes are modified to produce the best quality gourmet experiences at home with only a moderate degree of difficulty. You can find most of these ingredients at your local supermarket. A little shopping at specialty store will get you the rest.

Roast Pheasant with Grilled Corn, Madeira, and Chanterelle Mushrooms

    2 whole pheasants (skin on, aged)
    4 tablespoons butter
    1 teaspoon thyme (fresh or dried)
    Salt to taste (kosher or sea)
    Black pepper to taste

Sauce:

    1 pint fresh chanterelles
    2 ears fresh corn
      (roasted in the husk, then removed from cob)
    $\frac{1}{4}$ cup Madeira wine (Bual or Malmsy)
    3 cups rich chicken broth
    1 head roasted garlic (cloves separated)
    1 tablespoon finely minced shallots
    1 tablespoon butter (softened with flour)
    1 tablespoon flour
    Salt and pepper to taste

Stuff pheasants between meat and skin with butter and thyme. Season outside with sea salt and fresh-ground black pepper. Roast at 450°F to 475°F for twelve to eighteen minutes. Rest until room temperature. Carve breasts in half, remove drumsticks. Reheat pieces at 350°F to medium doneness. Serve thigh and half breast per person.

For the sauce, use a spoon to scrape any burnt meat drippings from pan, discard. Add shallots and cook slowly in bottom of pan with drippings. Remove excess butter and fat; discard. Turn heat up high and add chanterelles, sauté until tender, stirring frequently, so as not to burn the shallots and drippings on bottom of pan. Add Madeira and reduce off alcohol.

Add corn, chicken broth, and garlic cloves. Corn has natural starch and will lightly tighten sauce if simmered for a few minutes. Finish sauce by whisking flour-butter in until lumps disappear (but don't boil), approximately ten minutes. Salt and pepper to taste. Serve over sliced breast, leg, and thigh meat. Serves four.

ANCHO CHILI PAN-FRIED PHEASANT WITH SWEET POTATO MOLASSES PANCAKES

8 pieces pheasant breasts and thighs (skin on or off)
1 cup buttermilk
½ cup flour
¼ cup ancho chili (fresh-ground powder)
Peanut oil
1 tablespoon fresh garlic, minced fine
Salt to taste
Fresh ground black pepper to taste

Sauce:

Juice of 2 lemons
½ cup black beans (soaked)
3 cups chicken broth
2 cloves garlic
1 teaspoon cumin
1 bay leaf
3-4 dashes Tabasco
¼ teaspoon thyme
Salt and pepper to taste
¼ cup heavy cream
2 slices bacon

Add garlic to buttermilk. Mix flour, ancho-chili powder, salt, and pepper together. Soak pheasant in buttermilk-garlic mixture for three to four hours in refrigerator. Dip in flour- chili mixture, then pan-fry in peanut oil until crisp, and cook through. For sauce, sauté bacon, spices, and garlic until brown. Add drained black beans and sauté together five minutes. Add chicken broth, and cook beans on low heat until done. Take out bacon.

After removing bay leaf, puree beans in blender or food processor.

Pour in heavy cream; add salt, pepper, and Tabasco to taste. Serve with chili-fried pheasant. Note: If beans become overly thick, thin with more broth.

SWEET POTATO AND MOLASSES PANCAKES

2 sweet potatoes
¼ cup finely minced leeks
1½ tablespoons molasses
1 whole egg
Salt and pepper to taste
Butter for frying

Peel and grate sweet potatoes. Briefly par-cook grated sweet potato and leek together by steaming until sweet potato has just started to turn soft. Cool to room temperature and add molasses, egg, salt, and pepper. Press into thin silver-dollar-sized pancakes and slowly sauté until golden brown; arrange around chili-fried pheasant with black bean sauce. Serves four to six.

CONFIT OF PHEASANT

3 cups olive oil
   (pommace or light style, not virgin style)
4 cloves garlic
3 bay leaves
1 teaspoon thyme
6 pieces leg and thigh meat
¼ cup sea salt
3 whole cloves

Sprinkle legs and thighs with salt and cloves, refrigerate for four hours. Rinse well with cold water until all traces of salt have been removed. Pat dry until no water is left on meat. Combine oil, meat, seasoning, and spice mixture in a heavy-gauge saucepan and simmer for approximately one and one-half hours. Only allow oil to bubble very gently, since you are actually poaching in fat. *Warning:* High heat will deep-fry the meat. Instead, simmer in oil, cooking until fork tender. Strain, reserving oil for another confit, then refrigerate. *Note:* Employ confit as a base to utilize leg and thigh meat. The meat can be flaked and tossed in pasta or salad. It makes an easy pizza topping, and is also excellent when served on the bone with sautéed or roasted breasts and your favorite sauce.

PHEASANT WITH MORELS AND SHERRY

8 breasts or thighs of pheasant
1 ounce dried morel mushrooms
 (rinsed quickly in cold water)
1 cup dry sherry
2 finely minced shallots
$\frac{1}{4}$ teaspoon nutmeg
1 teaspoon fresh lemon juice
1 pint heavy cream (unsweetened)
$\frac{1}{2}$ cup pearl onions, peeled
1 tablespoon butter
Salt and white pepper to taste

Season breasts and legs with salt and pepper, then sear with butter in iron skillet or heavy-gauge sauté pan. Remove breasts from pan and sauté pearl onions until dark golden brown. Add minced shallots and cook briefly, making sure not to burn. Add sherry to same pan and reduce by half. Transfer to heavy-gauge sauce pan (not larger than two quarts) and add heavy cream, sautéed pheasant, and rinsed morels. *Note:* Dried morels rehydrate in the sauce, adding intense flavor and thickening it as well. Simmer on low heat. Add lemon juice and nutmeg; salt and pepper to taste. When sauce has thickened and meat is tender, serve.

PHEASANT BREAST WITH PORT AND SOUR CHERRY SAUCE

4 pheasant breasts (skin on)
Salt and pepper to taste
½ cup dried sour cherries
¾ cup port wine (Warres Warrior, Fonesca Bin 27)
1 ½ cups chicken broth
1 tablespoon butter, softened
1 tablespoon flour (mix with butter)
1 tablespoon finely minced shallots

Sauté pheasant breasts until medium brown. Take breasts out of pan and let cool to room temperature. Add shallots and cook at low temperature until opaque. Add port, reduce by half; slowly add chicken broth, reduce by half. Add sour cherries and cook until firm but tender; strain half the rehydrated cherries out and chop fine with a French knife. Add semi-puréed cherry mixture to sauce again and slowly cook to simmer. Finish with butter-flour mixture, whisked in until all lumps dissolve. Simmer ten minutes (do not boil) and serve over sautéed pheasant breast. Serves four.

JAY JOHNSON

Pheasants Forever was formed in 1982 to protect pheasants and other wildlife throughout North America.

Jay Johnson has served as the organization's Special Projects Director since 1987. He lives in Forest Lake, Minnesota, north of St. Paul.

For more information on Pheasants Forever, write to P.O. Box 75473, St. Paul, MN 55175, or call 612-481-7142.

thirteen

PHEASANTS FOREVER

by Jay Johnson

Pheasants Forever. As hunters, we certainly hope so. To over 70,000 sportsmen and women, our name is also a rallying cry to join the fight to preserve the king of farmland game birds.

Pheasants Forever was formed in 1982 for the sole purpose of empowering local hunters with the knowledge and tools necessary to upgrade pheasant habitat and, in turn, increase pheasant populations. To accomplish this, we have initiated programs of habitat improvement, public awareness and education, and land management that benefits farmers and wildlife alike.

Pheasants Forever comprises a unique system of county chapters that provide an incentive for sportsmen and women to raise money: most of the funds raised by chapters remain at the chapter level for use in implementation of local habitat projects and conservation education. Chapter leaders, with the help of resource professionals, establish habitat, conservation, and education programs customized to meet the needs in their area. This enables local supporters to see direct results from their contributions of time and money. A typical chapter habitat-restoration program might include one or all of the following elements: nesting cover establishment, winter cover plantings of windbreaks, food plot establishments, wetland restorations, and critical habitat acquisitions.

The importance of educating the public about the needs of pheasants and other wildlife cannot be overstated. Pheasants Forever is therefore committed to public-awareness programs, and places special emphasis on the conservation education of children. Through our innovative Kids for Pheasants program, we are helping to ensure the continuation of our nation's hunting and outdoor legacies.

Pheasants Forever also initiates and supports both federal and state conservation legislation benefiting the ringneck and other wildlife, and has been instrumental in developing and implementing state pheasant-stamp-habitat-improvement programs, and in continuing and improving critical conservation provisions in the 1995 Farm Bill.

As I sit at my keyboard this afternoon typing these words, the powers that be in Washington, D.C., are forging the details for the conservation provisions that will be included as part of the 1995 Farm Bill. This is important because federal agricultural policy has, for the past five decades, dictated land use and agricultural production, and the pheasant has served as a barometer of the land's health in response to the legislative process. In general, legislation aimed at boosting crop production has been detrimental to wildlife populations. On the other hand, programs that seek to curtail crop production through long-term land-retirement programs like CRP have been beneficial. It all comes down to having adequate habitat and meeting the birds' living requirements.

To forecast the future for pheasants one need only look at the past. Changes in farming practices that alter the face of the landscape have caused pheasant populations to either peak or plummet.

Initiated in 1956, the Soil Bank Program retired over 27 million acres of cropland. As a result, by the early 1960s our nation's pheasant population reached a near-record high. Whenever we compare the hunting of today with that of yesteryear, my dad fondly recalls the incredible pheasant hunting of the Soil Bank days. That's not unusual. For most hunters, the pheasant hunting of the late 1950s and early 1960s is the benchmark by which all subsequent hunting is measured.

Then came the 1970s and the infamous fencerow-to-fencerow farming policy espoused by Secretary of Agriculture Earl Butz. The Soil Bank Program had ended and all the acreage the program had retired went back into production. Moreover, many landowners found it necessary to attempt to farm some of the marginal land they owned just to stay in business. The bottom line was this: as the land was more intensely farmed, pheasant populations reached record lows.

I grew up pheasant hunting in Minnesota during the 1970s, so Dad and I spent a lot of time walking without seeing birds. Many pheasant hunters gave up, directing their sporting interest elsewhere. For pheasants and pheasant hunters, that was an hour as dark as the black fields plowed fencerow to fencerow.

The early 1980s didn't look much better. Severe winter weather coupled with a lack of cover across a major portion of the pheasant range had driven bird numbers down considerably. But those who were paying attention to changes occurring in agricultural policy saw hope on the horizon. They recognized in the changes the potential to resuscitate ringneck populations and thereby jump-start hunters' interest in pheasants.

The biggest change came in the form of the 1985 Farm Bill's Conservation Reserve Program (CRP), which idled close to 38 million acres of farmland. It was the Soil Bank days all over again; the pheasant population rebounded dramatically. In many areas, landscape that had been nothing more than a mosaic of corn and soybean fields was suddenly transformed into the perfect mix of grassland and cropland. As a result, local pheasant populations exploded.

Hunting near Marshalltown, Iowa, in 1988, Rick Piefer and I, along with our yearling setters, found pheasants in numbers that rivaled any stories I'd heard about the good old days! Taking a three-bird limit over our young dogs was only the icing on the cake. The real thrill came from just being in the country with so many birds. The area was laced with large blocks of CRP grasslands, and on any given day during that spectacular season we could see literally hundreds of pheasants.

Since then, I've witnessed the same scene in farmlands from Kansas to North Dakota. The bottom line: habitat is the key to wildlife abundance. The idled acres created through CRP have pushed pheasant numbers to their highest levels since the early 1960s.

So you ask, what does the future hold for pheasants? The future depends on the direction federal policy takes in the twenty-first century. If the American farming machine is turned loose on a campaign to maximize crop production, the pheasant population will plummet. If, on the other hand, we can maintain a balance between crop production and habitat concerns, the future for pheasants and other wildlife looks bright.

Equally important is the need to pass on the heritage of pheasant hunting to the next generation.

Every year the average age of hunters increases. Next time you're having breakfast at the local cafe in pheasant country, make a mental note of the age of your pheasant hunting peers. Statistical surveys tell us that, on average, today's pheasant hunter is over forty years old. Which doesn't surprise me. At 35, I'm normally the youngest among the group I hunt with.

Young men and women are not being recruited into the ranks of pheasant hunters. As the latest in a long line of hunters who were taught the love of the hunt by preceding generations, we have dropped the ball in passing our heritage to today's youth.

Granted, every year it seems to be more and more difficult to get kids out into the field. Children and their families find themselves pulled in many directions. Free time is limited. Many of us, for that matter, find that the actual amount of time available to engage in activities such as hunting has decreased. Add to this the problems of land access and the cost factors involved in hunting, and it's no wonder we see fewer young people afield.

In spite of the obstacles that stand in our way, it is critical to foster a passion for the hunt in today's youth. This passion will ultimately be the basis on which they stand when fighting for and implementing future wildlife conservation policy.

Maybe it's time for us to implement a national adopt-a-young-hunter program. Whether it's your son, daughter, or the kid who cuts your grass, next time you're going on a hunt, invite them along—even if at first it's only to walk and observe. If you're like me, you'll find that bringing a youngster into the world of hunting, and watching their sense of wonderment as they learn about the nature, is ample reward for you efforts.

Pheasants forever. Pheasant hunters. The two go hand-in-hand. The efforts of both are absolutely critical to the future of our sport. It's our responsibility to see that our pheasant hunting heritage is fortified and passed on to future generations.

JOHN MADSON

"Pheasants Beyond Autumn" was first published almost twenty years ago, not long after I first met John Madson. John was the finest sporting and natural-history writer of his generation, and a much-treasured friend right up until his death in 1995.

A native Iowan like myself, John loved pheasants. To him, a sly old rooster was the ultimate game bird, and no one could capture the essence of pheasant hunting quite the way he could.

When I started putting together the book, John Madson: Out Home, in the late 1970s, "Pheasants Beyond Autumn" was the first chapter I chose. I'd always thought it was the single best pheasant piece I'd ever read—and I haven't seen anything since to change my mind.

Michael McIntosh

fourteen

PHEASANTS BEYOND AUTUMN

by John Madson

here is a dichotomy in pheasant hunting, as in any hunting that is worth doing. There are sets of paired contrasts: two pheasant seasons, two kinds of hunters, two types of birds. Gold and gray, gay and grim, yin and yang.

One pheasant season may last no longer than opening weekend—a brief, burnished time with Indian summer still on the land, the afternoons soft, and tawny hunters with their coats open. The other pheasant season is quieter and grayer, reaching far into December. The sky is often stone-colored then, filled with prairie winds that cut with a wire edge, and even on clear days the sunlight is pale and without substance.

In that first season there were hunters by the hundreds of thousands, sweeping the fields in wide lines with deployed blockers,

181

plaguing farmers and each other, shooting at pheasants hopelessly far away, ripping out the crotches of new hunting pants on bobwire fences, and generally having a helluva time. They head back to town with or without birds, often making a stop along the way and arriving home late and smelling like hot mince pies. They are not likely to reappear on the landscape for about one year.

The pheasant hunters who do return, and keep returning, have a singular worn quality. Their canvas coats are likely to be weatherstained and shapeless, with the main button missing and a pronounced sag in the region of the game pocket, and their gunmetal is worn to the white. They hunt without haste—dire men in twos and threes, or often alone with an old retriever at heel. Men shaped and colored by circumstance, as fitted to their environment as horseweeds and cockleburs—and just as enduring and tenacious. They must be, to match the birds they now hunt.

The pheasants of the opening weekend were overwhelmingly birds of the year, callow juveniles that rose clattering into the air within easy gun range. Those birds went home with the opening-day hunters and, like them, will not reappear for another year. The birds that remain are sagacious old roosters with long spurs, or smart young cocks that won their spurs during the first week of hunting. Such pheasants have much in common with the remaining hunters. Each tempers and hones the other in a process of mutual refinement.

There is some loss of pheasants with the first intense shock of cold weather. There is a marked loss of hunters as well. By then both pheasant and hunter have evolved beyond their opening-day counterparts—for it needs a tougher breed of hunter to pit himself against the pheasant range of late December, and a tougher breed of pheasant to resist him. But somehow, the pheasant tends to harden and sharpen a bit ahead of the man who hunts him, even the very good man. There comes a point where hunter persistence is outstripped by pheasant resistance—and the roosters always win.

The December pheasant is the real pheasant and to hunt him is to hunt pheasants truly. Which is not to say that opening weekend is unworthy of serious regard. It is a very special time, a season apart, that late October or early November opening. A wedding party and honeymoon in one—green and golden preface to a hardworking marriage between bird and gunner.

Opening day is when a small boy is allowed to tag along for the first time and maybe even carry Dad's first rooster of the day, and get to keep the tailfeathers. The boy will soon be carrying a 20-bore and rooster of his own.

It is a time when the clans gather, when old hunting pards rendezvous. They come from all compass points, reaffirming the faith. I'll go home to central Iowa again and hook up with Harry Harrison or Skeeter Wheeler. Or Glen Yates—leathery, irascible,

ornery, deeply regarded Yates. Sly old cuss Yates, with his bib overalls and tattered coat and sweet 16, and a profound and abiding knowledge of the ring-necked pheasant. Opening day is playday for us. Gooney bird day, time to test the young roosters and see how all the folks are doing out there in the fields. As Yates put it: "Of course opening day ain't pheasant hunting. Hell, that ain't new. But it's the start of it—and Kee-rist, Madseen, am I ready!"

It's this opening day that largely supports wildlife conservation in much of the Midwest—notably Iowa, Kansas, Nebraska, and south Dakota. License sales soar just before the pheasant season, swelling the game and fish coffers while gun and ammunition receipts build the Pittman-Robertson fund. In Iowa, about 300,000 residents buy hunting licenses. About 290,00 of them hunt pheasants—and probably 80 percent are out there on the great Saturday. If there were no pheasant opening in Iowa, as many as 200,000 licenses might go unsold in a given year—and the wildlife conservation program would go down the tube. It is much the same elsewhere. Let us look kindly on opening day.

A lot of bird hunting isn't really hunting. For example, you don't hunt waterfowl and wild turkey. You seduce and delude them. Nor do men usually hunt quail. They hunt for the dog that's hunting for the quail.

Early-season pheasant hunting isn't likely to be hunting so much as just combing through cover. Birds are likely to be almost anywhere in the early November fields and edges, so it's usually a matter of just pointing yourself at the general landscape and grinding out mileage.

But later pheasant hunting may be as pure a form of hunting as there is. The hunter then becomes a classic searcher and stalker, shooting less and hunting much, much more. There are still a few ribbon clerks trying to shoot pheasants from cars—but that's a pallid imitation of sport that doesn't rally produce much. While the pheasant season is still young, the birds have begun to shrink away from roadsides. The slow ones are dead, and most of the others are likely to be somewhere back in the fields where things are more peaceful. (With exceptions, of course. We know a man who hunts late-season birds in the thick brome of certain Interstate-80 interchanges. He says he does all right. As near as we can figure it, the only law he's breaking is the one prohibiting pedestrians on the interstate highways.)

I don't have much late-season cunning, but one practice that's worked out well is simply getting as far as possible from roads. An obvious reason is that most birds have faded away from roadside field edges. Ten, too, the very center of a square-mile section of midwestern cornland may be the untidiest part. It's where the farmer tends to sweep stuff under the rug, back where passersby can't see small farm dumps, weed patches, messy fencerows, and junk machinery.

I once found a mile-square section whose exact center was low and boggy, and whose owner had never gone to the expense and effort of extending tile lines from there to the nearest road ditch a half mile away. Since the swale was probably lower than the distant road ditch, drainage wouldn't have been possible, anyway. The result was a little two-acre oasis that was abandoned to wild grasses and forbs. And pheasants, of course. Unless a man stood on the cab of his pick-up truck (which I did), this could not be seen from the road.

In contrast is a certain square mile of central Iowa farm-land that lies on a terminal moraine. In most of my home country a man can plow all day and not see a stone bigger than a walnut, but this particular township has sprinklings of glacial erratics. Over the years, farmers had removed such debris from their fields to a slight lift of land in the center of my hunting ground, where today a modest boulder field covers almost an acre—together with several rolls of old fencing and a mantle of goldenrod, lesser ragweed, and sumac. This little niche is a magnet for wildlife, although I never hit it hard nor often. Once a season is enough.

Out here in corn country—and about everywhere else—a man must exploit two extremes in his late-season pheasant hunting. He must hunt close and far, alternating between dense coverts and wide, naked fields.

There are genuine pheasant hunters who think nothing of reducing new canvas pants to shredded rags in the course of a single hunting season. They churn around in terrible places—deep pockets of raspberry canes undergrown with dense grass, rough weedy creek banks thick with catbriar tangles, and the steep banks of old bullditches with their overgrowth of ragweed and sumac. You know—the kinds of cover that hurt just to look at. But these are the haunts of late-season roosters, and the men who rout them out of such stuff do so with the premise that the only places worth hunting in late-season are in cover that no sane man would ever enter.

Such attention to detail, and willingness to suffer for it, applies to open field gunning as well. It may mean hunting in rough plowing, such as plowed pastures where broken sod is left to mellow over the winter. These are the devil's own fields to walk in; the black surfaces of the upturned sods become as slippery as grease during the midday thaw, and a man can break his bones there. Still, roosters may be sheltering in a sun-warmed hollows between and under the big clods, and a hunter must go where the birds may be. If there's any comfort in this, it's knowing that pheasants are as reluctant to run in heavy plowing as men are. Well, almost.

This breed of hunter will turn aside from a comfortable fenceline and stumble across a quarter of plowing to hunt a wisp of grassed waterway only a few yards long, or walk hundreds of yards out of his way to investigate a basket-sized tuft of foxtail in a picked cornfield, or a distant hay bale that the farmer failed to pick up. No cover feature in the barren winter landscape is too minor to overlook. It is hunting based on three articles of faith: 1) that much of the pre-season rooster population is still out there, and although 2) there is no cheap late-season pheasant, 3) the longer you hunt without flushing a bird, the closer you are to flushing one.

Pheasants range more widely in winter than at any other time of year. They are constantly adjusting to impending storms, snow-choked roosts, and deep cold and wind. Vagaries of wind and snow drifting will eliminate certain niches of the birds' range, and bring others into play. Marvelously rugged and adaptable birds, winter pheasants never cease probing and exploring.

Aldo Leopold observed that Wisconsin pheasants were sometimes restless in coverts of less than ten acres. Where small coverts prevailed, pheasants were likely to adopt a winter "circuit-type" movement, traveling from one covert to another in a sequence spreading over a mile of distance and several days' time. Leopold believed that Wisconsin pheasants in good winter range had an average cruising radius of one-eighth to one-half mile, and two or three miles at the most.

Since today's winter coverts in the primary range are almost always less than ten acres, such fiddle-footed drifting may be a common trait in many regions. Although a particular covert may not hold birds today, it doesn't mean that they might not be there tomorrow or a couple of days from now. On the contrary, it could mean that they probably will be.

Our most successful wild birds and mammals are those that have not been fixed in rigid frames of specialization, but are generalized in design and function. The pheasant is a pretty good example of this, owing much of his success to a rather generalized form and knack for ready adjustment. We can't really ascribe much intelligence to the pheasant. After all, the chicken tribe wasn't at the head of the line when brains were passed out. But the ringneck is certainly "country smart"; he may not know his way to town, but he sure ain't lost. He develops a remarkably shrewd sense of range. Not as well as the red fox or white-tailed deer, perhaps, but infinitely better than the men who hunt him there.

We human hunters are likely to regard countryside in terms of drainage systems and patterns of cultivation and habitation. Or, at best, in terms of entire brushy creeks, dry sloughs, and weedy fields. Wild hunted creatures like the pheasant learn their native heath in terms of minute, intimate crannies—little sections of overhung creek bank, the tree stump covered with vines and weeds, that old roll of fence wire smothered with giant foxtail. Our eyes are always about six feet above the ground; the pheasant's are down there among the details, down in the tangled heart of the covert, and an instant later his eyes may be forty feet in the air. A pheasant is exposed to the major and minor feature of his home range in ways that the hunter can never hope to be, and he is highly capable of exploiting that exposure in stress situations.

While trading from one major winter covert to another, a pheasant is about as likely to walk as fly. In the course of such commuting he continually adds to his experience bank. If the obvious winter hangouts are regularly disturbed by hunters, many ringnecks begin to rely on interim coverts—little pockets of sanctuary that they have happened upon along the way. This occurs too often to be a fluke—occasions when certain birds are not to be found in any conventional shelter-belt or weedy slough, but are shut down in the weedy mouth of an old culvert or in a snug form of tented bluegrass in an orchard. The complete pheasants hunter must learn to think in such terms. This is one of the reasons that I enjoy hunting pheasant on snow. It's all written out there, although I often fail to comprehend what I read.

It's on snow that one can trace daily feeding patterns, some of winter circuitry between far-flung coverts, and the bewildering and often admirable interactions of winter pheasants and their harsh world. Such tracking is more likely to instruct in natural history than to result in shooting. My lifetime success rate for converting pheasant tracks to Sunday dinners can't be much more than 2 percent. Something usually goes wrong.

But if I've learned one thing about trailing, it's this: to never think in terms of a pheasant resting placidly at the end of a line of tracks. If those tracks are really fresh, the pheasant is almost certainly aware of being trailed and you will rarely get a shot while the bird is on the move. It's his pausing-place that you must find. If the trail appears to lead across rather open ground to a distant pocket of weedy cover, swing far to the side and come in from behind. I think this may be the only way I've ever trailed and killed pheasants—by leaving the trail and flanking the bird at some point ahead. Several times, on fresh snow, I have found the roosters had entered bits of cover and had hooked around in order to watch their backtrails.

Snow lends certain advantages to the pheasant hunter. Birds can be more easily seen in distant feeder fields and coverts in snowtime, crippled birds can be readily trailed, and dead pheasants are easier to find in heavy cover. Yet, snowtime is hardly a situation in which the callused gunner exploits a vulnerable population and kills pheasants at will. My success rate at tracking and shooting pheasants on snow is about the same as my fox-trailing with a rifle—reinforcing my long-held conviction that the ring-necked pheasant is nothing less than a feathered fox.

There's something I miss in my late-season hunting these days. For years I have begun pheasant hunts on wheels instead of legs, leaving home in a car or truck, driving as many miles as necessary, and returning in comfort. The day that I began to do this marked the end of my boyhood and pushed back the prairie horizons, but it wasn't necessarily progress.

It will never be like just stepping off the back stoop and loading my gun, walking across the garden, and being in hunting grounds almost at once. Pure hunting, that was, from home den out into the coverts and back to den again, like a young fox. It was never diluted, as now, with synthetic beginnings and highways.

Each cover patch would point to one beyond until I had overextended myself as I always did, and night had found me far from home. There is a keen and poignant quality in being a famished boy far afield with night coming on and miles of crusted snow yet to negotiate, the pheasants hanging over your shoulder with their legs tied with binder twine, and the little Monkey Ward double gun beginning to weigh heavy. (I had bought the gun's mismatched 16-gauge shells at Walsh's Hardware, out of a bin where they were all mixed together and served up like rock candy—three cents apiece and you took what came up in the scoop, with no picking over the shells for preferred shot sizes or other such nonsense.)

Night coming on and glory lost, for there would be no daylight in which to parade past neighbor girls' houses, the bright roosters hung from my shoulder. The girls would never know what they had missed, but I would.

Now, for the first time in ten hours, a weakness beginning in the legs, and that exquisite knifelike stab high between the shoulder blades. Ten hours since oatmeal and coffee, with long crossings over plowed ground, and ranging through horseweed thickets laced with wild plum and raspberry canes, through fallow pastures of heavy tented grass, creekside willow slaps, over the high fields and under the bluffs, and into little cattail sloughs whose icy floors were skeined with pheasant tracks. And once, a half-mile dash along a crusted fenceline trying to flush a running rooster and failing to, gasping in the cold air and coughing for an hour afterward.

My lips and nose would be raw and sore from hours of wiping them with the backs of woolen mittens that a were quickly frozen. There was a winter twilight when I stopped and leaned against an old wolf cottonwood to rest, and took off my woolen stocking cap to mop my sore nose. It was the first time since morning that I'd taken off the cap; when I ran my fingers through my matted hair it protested at being disturbed, and I remember thinking it was funny that even my hair should hurt, but not funny enough to laugh about.

The wind freshening, swinging into the northwest and freighted with the smell of new snow. By now my corduroy pants are frozen to the knees, as stiff as stovepipes and rattling against each other and against the shoepacs that I had bought with my first fur check the year before. One foot ahead of the other, breaking through snow crust at each step, the slung birds cutting through the sheepskin coat and into thin shoulder, and a sort of homesickness growing at the sight of each lighted kitchen window in farmhouses across the fields. And finally, up ahead in the gathering darkness, a square of yellow reflecting on snow, strangely warm and vivid after the long hours of unrelieved white and gray. There ahead, a circle of light and warmth for a young hunter come home on a winter evening, late in pheasant season.

At last, up the back steps and out of the wild night into the rich kitchen smell of home, where pot roast with whole onions and carrots and potatoes is waiting on the back of the stove, and butter-crusted rolls still hot, with much-loved voices laughing and half-scolding and the close comfort of it wrapping a boy like a grandmother's quilt. I would take off coat and mittens before I began eating—but only because my mother forced me to. And soon to sleep, out in the back room with its icy linoleum, mounded over with lamb's-wool comforters and fleecy blankets smelling of cedar, the deep guiltless slumber of a hunter who has spent everything that he had of himself, and hunted as well as he knew how.

Just being young was part of this, of course, and coming home was a part of it, too. But there was more—a wild purity of hunting with all the fat rendered away, and reduced to the clean white bone. It was a closing of the magic circle of man, animal, and land, and once a boy glimpses this he remembers it all of his days.

This is the essence for which I will always hunt, for I often misplace it and seem seldom able to find it in the old full measure that I knew. But when it's found, it will likely be on some iron prairie at the knell of the year, with a cunning old ringneck out ahead and showing me the way.